Dorothea Ruggles-Brise, John Glen

Klers' Violin Repository of Dance Music

Vol. 3

Dorothea Ruggles-Brise, John Glen

Klers' Violin Repository of Dance Music
Vol. 3

ISBN/EAN: 9783337428167

Printed in Europe, USA, Canada, Australia, Japan

Cover: Foto ©Thomas Meinert / pixelio.de

More available books at **www.hansebooks.com**

Book Third

KÖHLERS'

VIOLIN REPOSITORY

OF

DANCE MUSIC,

COMPRISING

Reels, Strathspeys, Hornpipes, Country Dances,

QUADRILLES, WALTZES, &c.

EDITED BY

A PROFESSIONAL PLAYER.

EDINBURGH: ERNEST KÖHLER & SON, MUSICSELLERS, 11 NORTH BRIDGE.

MORISON BROTHERS, 99 BUCHANAN STREET, GLASGOW.

MARTIN, ABERDEEN.   MENZIES & CO., EDINBURGH.

J. CUNNINGHAM, DUNDEE.   J. M. MILLER, PERTH.   WILLIAM DEAS, KIRKCALDY.

JAMES HORSBURGH, 73 GEORGE STREET, DUNEDIN, NEW ZEALAND.

LONDON: CATTY & DOBSON, 14 PILGRIM ST., LUDGATE HILL.

CONTENTS.

UP IN THE MORNING EARLY—Variations.
Bowing and Fingering arranged by W. B. LAYBOURN.

Fine.

VERMONT HORNPIPE.

TITUS HORNPIPE.

ROSS HORNPIPE.

∨ Up Bow.   ⊓ Down Bow.

KÖHLER'S "VIOLIN REPOSITORY," 11 NORTH BRIDGE, EDINBURGH.

BUSHWICK HORNPIPE.

LONG ISLAND HORNPIPE.

HOWARD HORNPIPE.

∨ Up Bow. ⊓ Down Bow.

KÖHLERS' "VIOLIN REPOSITORY," 11 NORTH BRIDGE, EDINBURGH.

THE BANKS OF LOCH NESS—Strathspey.

D.C.

Segue Reel.

THE WEDDING RING REEL.

D.C.

"NEW YEAR'S DAY" STRATHSPEY.

D.C.

Segue Reel.

∨ Up Bow.   ⁝ ⁝ Two Up or Down Bows.

KÜHLERS' "VIOLIN REPOSITORY," 11 NORTH BRIDGE, EDINBURGH.

"CATCH AND KISS THE ROMP"—Reel.

D.C.

RINETTAN'S DAUGHTER—Strathspey.

D.C.

Segue Reel.

"THE PIPE SLANG"—Reel.

D.C.

∨ Up Bow.   ⊓ Down Bow.   ⌐⌐ Two Up or Down Bows.

KÖHLERS' "VIOLIN REPOSITORY," 11 NORTH BRIDGE, EDINBURGH.

LES FARCEURS VALSE. *Par* J. N. Hoglen, *Edinburgh.*

∨ Up Bow.   ⊓ Down Bow.   •⸺• Two Up or Down Bows.

Köhler's "Violin Repository," 11 North Bridge, Edinburgh.

V Up Bow.   ⊓ Down Bow.   ⌣ Two Up or Down Bows.

KÜHLERS' "VIOLIN REPOSITORY," 11 NORTH BRIDGE, EDINBURGH.

"THE FAIRY WEDDING" POLKA.

INTRODUCTION.

By W. C. PATON.

POLKA.

1st time. 2nd time.

JOHN O' GROATS JIG.

By JOHN BAIN, *Wick.*

ᐯ Up Bow.   ⊓ Down Bow.   ⌐——⌐ Two Up or Down Bows.

KÖHLERS' "VIOLIN REPOSITORY," 11 NORTH BRIDGE, EDINBURGH.

KÖHLERS' VIOLIN REPOSITORY.

No 26.]   PRICE 4D.   [COPYRIGHT.

A MUCH-ADMIRED GERMAN VALSE.

Bowing and Fingering arranged by W. B. LAYBOURN.

A FRENCH VALSE.

∨ Up Bow.   ∙——∙ Two Up or Down Bows.

KÖHLERS' "VIOLIN REPOSITORY," 11 NORTH BRIDGE, EDINBURGH.

CORNET HORNPIPE.

By W. P. Robertson, *Riccarton, Kilmarnock.*

WALKER STREET HORNPIPE.

D.C.

WORRELL'S HORNPIPE.

∨ Up Bow.

Köhlers' "Violin Repository," 11 North Bridge, Edinburgh.

JOHNSTON'S HORNPIPE.

THOMPSON'S HORNPIPE.

D.C.

MILLER'S HORNPIPE.

By ZEKE BACUS.

ᴠ Up Bow.   ⊓ Down Bow.

KÜHLERS' "VIOLIN REPOSITORY," 11 NORTH BRIDGE, EDINBURGH.

CORRYMONNY STRATHSPEY.

D.C.

BEAUFORT CASTLE REEL.

Segue Reel.

1st time.

D.C

HUNTLY'S WEDDING MEDLEY—Strathspey.

Fine.

D.C.

Segue Reel.

ᴠ Up Bow.   Two Up or Down Bows.

KÖHLERS' "VIOLIN REPOSITORY," 11 NORTH BRIDGE, EDINBURGH.

"MERRY MAY THE PAIR BE"—Reel.

"THE COCK OF THE NORTH"—Strathspey.

"FAIR FA' THE MINSTREL"—Reel.

∨ Up Bow. ⊓ Down Bow. ⌐——⌐ Two Up or Down Bows.

KÖHLERS' "VIOLIN REPOSITORY," 11 NORTH BRIDGE, EDINBURGH.

"THE NEW CONQUEST"—Contre Dance.

PADDY O' SNAP JIG—Contre Dance.

MISS SAMUEL'S FANCY JIG—Contre Dance.

D.C. for Finale.

∨ Up Bow.   ⊓ Down Bow.   ‗‗ Two Up or Down Bows.
KÖHLERS' "VIOLIN REPOSITORY," 11 NORTH BRIDGE, EDINBURGH.

BLACK JOCK, WITH VARIATIONS—*(To be Continued)*.

(To play this, tune the 3rd and 4th Strings one note higher than usual.)

Arranged by W. B. LAYBOURN.

$\vee$ Up Bow.   Two Up or Down Bows.

Volti Subito.

(Continued in next Number.)

∨ Up Bow.　　⊓ Down Bow.　　⌣ Two Up or Down Bows.

KÖHLERS' "VIOLIN REPOSITORY," 11 NORTH BRIDGE, EDINBURGH.

CONTINUATION OF BLACK JOCK—With Variations.

To play this, Tune the Third and Fourth Strings one note higher.

Arranged by W. B. LAYBOURN.

HALF SHIFT.

∨ Up Bow. ⊓ Down Bow. •—• Two Up or Down Bows.

KÖHLERS' "VIOLIN REPOSITORY," 11 NORTH BRIDGE, EDINBURGH.

CELIA SCHOTTISCHE.

JOHN TAYLOR.

V Up Bow.   ⊓ Down Bow.   ⌣ Two Up or Down Bows.

Köhlers' "Violin Repository," 11 North Bridge, Edinburgh.

THE THISTLE HORNPIPE.

BLUE BONNETS HORNPIPE.

THE SHAMROCK HORNPIPE. *By* W. C. Paton, *Edinr.*

V Up Bow.　　　＝＿＿＝ Two Up or Down Bows.

Köhlers' "Violin Repository," 11 North Bridge, Edinburgh.

FORGET-ME-NOT HORNPIPE. By J. C. PATON, *Edinburgh.*

ROCK HORNPIPE.

STETSON'S HORNPIPE.

∨ Up Bow.

KÜHLERS' "VIOLIN REPOSITORY," 11 NORTH BRIDGE, EDINBURGH.

JEANIE IN THE GLEN STRATHSPEY—(New.)

By J. M'QUEEN, Forres.

D.C.

Segue Reel.

JEANIE'S REEL. By W. B. LAYBOURN, from the above.

D.C.

FINALE.

M'QUEEN'S FROLIC—Strathspey.   By GEO. J. INGRAM.

D.C.

Segue Reel.

ᴠ Up Bow.   ᴖ——ᴖ Two Up or Down Bows.

KÖHLERS' "VIOLIN REPOSITORY," 11 NORTH BRIDGE, EDINBURGH.

THE SMIDDY'S CLAMOUR REEL—(New).

By J. M'QUEEN, Forres.

FINE.

CALDER'S WELCOME—Strathspey—(New).

By J. M'QUEEN, Forres.

D.C.

Segue Reel.

MRS. SCOTT SKINNER—Reel.

By J. M'QUEEN, Forres.

1st time.   2nd time.

D.C.

FINE.

∨ Up Bow.   ‿ Two Up or Down Bows.

PUBLISHED BY E. KÖHLER & SON, 11 NORTH BRIDGE, EDINBURGH.

WEISBADEN POLKA.

(To be Continued.)

∨ Up Bow.　　⊓ Down Bow.　　‿‿ Two Up or Down Bows.
KÖHLERS' "VIOLIN REPOSITORY," 11 NORTH BRIDGE, EDINBURGH.

EMELINA POLKA.

Bowing and Fingering arranged by W. B. LAYBOURN.

Introduction. *Vivace.*   *Composed by J. O. Paton, Edinburgh.*

Polka.

Trio.

mp dolce.

| 1st time. | 2nd time. |

Da Capo to :S:

WEE BELLA SCHOTTISCHE.

Composed by W. B. Laybourn.

| 1st time. | 2nd time. |

∨ Up Bow.   ⊓ Down Bow.   Two Up or Down Bows.

Köhlers' "Violin Repository," 11 North Bridge, Edinburgh.

CRAIGMILLAR CASTLE STRATHSPEY. *By W. O. Paton, Edinburgh.*

Segue Reel.

CRAIGMILLAR CASTLE REEL. *By W. O. Paton, Edinburgh.*

Finale.

CAIRDS O' KEITH STRATHSPEY. *By J. M'Queen, Forres.*

∨ Up Bow.　⊓ Down Bow.　Two Up or Down Bows.

Kühlers' "Violin Repository," 11 North Bridge, Edinburgh.

219

TO MY BED I WINNA GANG—Reel.

Fine.

"BALMORAL" STRATHSPEY. *Composed by W. B. Laybourn, 1884.*

D.C.

KEEP THE COUNTRY, BONNIE LASSIE.

V Up Bow. ⊓ Down Bow. Two Up or Down Bows.
Kühlers' "Violin Repository," 11 North Bridge, Edinburgh.

"THE CROWN" HORNPIPE. By W. C. Paton, Edinburgh.

"THE PEARL" HORNPIPE. By W. C. Paton, Edinburgh.

LENO HORNPIPE. Composed by J. Easton, Edinburgh.

V Up Bow. ∶―∶ Two Up or Down Bows.
Köhlers' "Violin Repository," 11 North Bridge, Edinburgh.

UNION JACK HORNPIPE. *Composed by* J. C. Paton, *Edinburgh*, 1884.

CAMPBELL'S HORNPIPE. *Composed by* W. B. Laybourn, *Edinburgh*, 1884.

HORNPIPE. *By* Archd. Allan, *Teacher of Dancing.*

∨ Up Bow. ∙——∙ Two Up or Down Bows.

Published by E. Köhler & Son, 11 North Bridge, Edinburgh.

THE LAIRD O' COCKPEN (for Two Violins).

PRIMO.

SECUNDO.

∨ Up Bow. ⊓ Down Bow. ⌣ Two Up or Down Bows,

KÖHLERS' "VIOLIN REPOSITORY," 11 NORTH BRIDGE, EDINBURGH.

THE LAIRD O' COCKPEN—Continued.

Fine.

v Up Bow. ⊓ Down Bow.

KÖHLERS' "VIOLIN REPOSITORY," 11 NORTH BRIDGE, EDINBURGH.

LORD HAWICK'S MARCH.

JAMES WARES', OF WICK, STRATHSPEY. *By* Jas. M'Queen, *Forres.*

ROSEBUD VALSE.

(To be Continued.)

∨ Up Bow.   ⊓ Down Bow.   ∙⌣∙ Two Up or Down Bows.
Kühlers' "Violin Repository," 11 North Bridge, Edinburgh.

KÖHLERS' VIOLIN REPOSITORY.

No 29.]   PRICE 4D.   [COPYRIGHT.

1. **OUR LITTLE BEAUTIES—Valse.** *Composed by* W. C. Paton.
Bowing and Fingering arranged by W. B. Laycourn.

V Up Bow.   ⊓ Down Bow.   ·—· Two Up or Down Bows.
KÖHLERS' "VIOLIN REPOSITORY," 11 NORTH BRIDGE, EDINBURGH.

4.

STARLIGHT SCHOTTISCHE.

By JAMES FRANCIS, *Edinburgh*, 1884.

2nd time 8ves.

D.C. Fine.

TRIO.

1st time. *2nd.*

D.C. Fine.

∨ Up Bow.   ⊓ Down Bow.   Two Up or Down Bows.

KÜHLERS' "VIOLIN REPOSITORY," 11 NORTH BRIDGE, EDINBURGH.

IMPERIAL HORNPIPE.

By James Francis, *Edinburgh*, 1884.

DAISY HORNPIPE.

By James Francis, *Edinburgh*, 1884.

∨ Up Bow.　⊓ Down Bow.　‿ Two Up or Down Bows.

KÖHLERS' "VIOLIN REPOSITORY," 11 NORTH BRIDGE, EDINBURGH.

RONDO.

Moderato.

By J. PLEYEL.

V Up Bow.   ⊓ Down Bow.   ⌣ Two Up or Down Bows.

KÖHLERS' "VIOLIN REPOSITORY," 11 NORTH BRIDGE, EDINBURGH.

RONDO—Continued.

V Up Bow. ⊓ Down Bow. –•–•– Two Up or Down Bows.

Köhlers' "Violin Repository," 11 North Bridge, Edinburgh.

THE DARLING STRATHSPEY.

Segue Reel.

ANNIE IS MY DARLING—Reel.

Fine.

THE EWIE WI' THE CROOKED HORN—Strathspey.

Segue Reel.

∨ Up Bow.   ⊓ Down Bow.   ⌣⌣ Two Up or Down Bows.
KÖHLERS' "VIOLIN REPOSITORY," 11 NORTH BRIDGE, EDINBURGH.

THE SCOLDING WIVES OF ABERTARFF—Reel.

D.C.

Fine.

MILLER LADS—Strathspey.

1st time.

2nd time.

1st time.

2nd time.

D.C.

Segue Reel.

INVERNESS LASSES—Reel.

1st time.

2nd time.

D.C.

Fine.

∨ Up Bow. ⊓ Down Bow. Two Up or Down Bows.

KÖHLERS' "VIOLIN REPOSITORY," 11 NORTH BRIDGE, EDINBURGH.

BOB, THE SAILOR, HORNPIPE.

MONTMORRIS HORNPIPE.

LIGHTFOOT HORNPIPE. *By* J. B. EASTON, *Edinburgh.*

(To be Continued.)

∨ Up Bow. ⊓ Down Bow. ⌐ ⌐ Two Up or Down Bows.

KÖHLERS' "VIOLIN REPOSITORY," 11 NORTH BRIDGE, EDINBURGH.

BUY A BROOM—Old German Air, with variations. *Arr. by* T. W. HOWARD.
Bowing and Fingering arranged by W. B. LAYBOURN.

AIR.

1st Variation.

2nd Variation.

3rd Variation.

Fine.

V Up Bow.   ⊓ Down Bow.   ‿ Two Up or Down Bows.

DAVIE MOFFAT'S HORNPIPE.

Composed by R. BAILLIE,
PETER BAILLIE'S GRANDSON, *Penicuick*.

THE PENICUICK HORNPIPE.

Composed by R. BAILLIE, *Penicuick*.

TOM TULLIE'S HORNPIPE—(Very Old).

D.C.

V Up Bow. ⊓ Down Bow. ⌣ Two Up or Down Bows.
KÖHLERS' "VIOLIN REPOSITORY," 11 NORTH BRIDGE, EDINBURGH.

MR. MARTON'S HORNPIPE.

LOCH LEVEN CASTLE HORNPIPE.

THE FINE OLD MAN versus GLADSTONE'S HORNPIPE.

Composed by W. B. LAYDOURN, *Edinburgh,* 1884.

∨ Up Bow.   ⊓ Down Bow.   ⸬ Two Up or Down Bows.

KÖHLERS' "VIOLIN REPOSITORY," 11 NORTH BRIDGE, EDINBURGH.

ROTHEMURCHUE'S RANT—Strathspey.

D.C.

Segue Reel.

THE MERRY LADS OF AYR—Reel.

Fine.

KINRARO'S STRATHSPEY.

MARSHALL.

Segue Reel.

D.C.

∨ Up Bow. ⊓ Down Bow. ⌣ Two Up or Down Bows.

PUBLISHED BY E. KÖHLER & SON, 11 NORTH BRIDGE, EDINBURGH.

GLEN FARNETE REEL.

Fine. *D.C.*

MRS. CAPTAIN STEWART'S, OF FINCASTLE, STRATHSPEY.

1st time. *2nd time.*

Segue Reel. *D.C.*

COLIN M'KAY'S REEL.

Fine.

V Up Bow.   ⊓ Down Bow.   ⌣ Two Up or Down Bows.

KÖHLERS' "VIOLIN REPOSITORY," 11 NORTH BRIDGE, EDINBURGH.

DUO POUR DEUX VIOLONS.

Andante.
VIOLINO PRIMO.

Par JAMES C. PATON.

AN OLD FAVOURITE MINUETTO.

Moderato.

PRIMO.

∨ Up Bow. ⊓ Down Bow. ▱ Two Up or Down Bows.

KÜHLERS' "VIOLIN REPOSITORY," 11 NORTH BRIDGE, EDINBURGH.

DUO POUR DEUX VIOLONS.

Andante.
VIOLINO SECONDO.

Par JAMES C. PATON.

A FAVOURITE MINUETTO.

Moderato.

VIOLINO SECONDO.

V Up Bow. ⊓ Down Bow. • — • Two Up or Down Bows.
PUBLISHED BY E. KÖHLER & SON, 11 NORTH BRIDGE, EDINBURGH.

TOM THUMB—Contre Dance.

JOHN DWIGHT'S PLANTATION DANCE.

DASHING WHITE SERGEANT—Contre Dance.

D.C.

Moderato. ## OWRE THE MUIR AMONG THE HEATHER—Variations.

(To be Continued.)

∨ Up Bow.   ⊓ Down Bow.   ⌐⌐ Two Up or Down Bows.

KÖHLERS' "VIOLIN REPOSITORY," 11 NORTH BRIDGE, EDINBURGH.

• 1.   **AERIAL QUADRILLE.**   *Composed by* J. SCOTT, Sandyholm, Lockerbie.
Bowing and Fingering arranged by W. B. LAYBOURN.

* *Staccato*—Heel of Bow, Nos. 1 and 3.
V Up Bow.   ⊓ Down Bow.   ⌐—⌐ Two Up or Down Bows.
PUBLISHED BY E. KÖHLER & SON, 11 NORTH BRIDGE, EDINBURGH.

4.

5.

SUNBEAM POLKA.

A. ANDERSON.

TRIO.

ⵎ *pp 1st, ff 2nd time.*

THE SHAMROCK HORNPIPE. *By* JOHN B. EASTON, Edinburgh.

MR. JAMES GRANT'S HORNPIPE. *By* WM. FINDLAY.

SIR GARNET'S HORNPIPE. *By* WM. FINDLAY.

V Up Bow.　　⊓ Down Bow.　　⌣ Two Up or Down Bows.

KÖHLERS' "VIOLIN REPOSITORY," 11 NORTH BRIDGE, EDINBURGH.

DONALD BUTCHER'S BRIDAL (with Variations).

∨ Up Bow. ⊓ Down Bow. ⌣ Two Up or Down Bows.

KÖHLERS' "VIOLIN REPOSITORY," 11 NORTH BRIDGE, EDINBURGH.

DONALD BUTCHER'S BRIDAL—*Continued.*

MISS HAMILTON'S STRATHSPEY.

Segue Reel.

LORD KELLIE'S REEL.

D.C.

Fine.

LADY ANN STEWART'S STRATHSPEY.

Segue Reel.

✳ First two Notes point of Bow, and the Slur whole Bow.

∨ Up Bow.   ⊓ Down Bow.   ⁓ Two Up or Down Bows.

KÜHLERS' "VIOLIN REPOSITORY," 11 NORTH BRIDGE, EDINBURGH.

247

LADY GRACE DOUGLAS'S REEL.

D.C.
Fine.

MR. MURRAY OF ABERCARNEY'S STRATHSPEY.

Segue Reel.

MR. MORTHLAND'S REEL.

D.C.
Fine.

V Up Bow. ⊓ Down Bow. ᴗ Two Up or Down Bows.
Köhlers' "Violin Repository," 11 North Bridge, Edinburgh.

COBORN'S DELIGHT HORNPIPE.

MOUNT SHASTA HORNPIPE.

1st time.   *2nd time.*   D.C.

OLD HICKORY HORNPIPE.

(To be Continued.)

⋁ Up Bow.   ⊓ Down Bow.   ⌐•⌐•⌐ Two Up or Down Bows.

PUBLISHED BY E. KÖHLER & SON, 11 NORTH BRIDGE, EDINBURGH.

KÖHLERS' VIOLIN REPOSITORY.

No 32.]   PRICE 4D.   [COPYRIGHT.

Newly out. **Set Waltzes—"GLENPATRICK,"** By JOHN B. EASTON, Edinburgh, 1884.
Bowing and Fingering arranged by W. B. LAYBOURN.

PRINCESS BEATRICE HORNPIPE. *Composed by* W. B. LAYBOURN, 1885.

ANNIE'S HORNPIPE. *Composed by* W. B. LAYBOURN, 1885.

1st time.   *2nd time.*

D.C.

DAVIE LONIE'S FARM YARD HORNPIPE.
Composed by W. B. LAYBOURN, Edinburgh, 1885.

D.C.

∨ Up Bow.   ⊓ Down Bow.   Two Up or Down Bows.

PUBLISHED BY E. KÖHLER & SON, 11 NORTH BRIDGE, EDINBURGH.

MRS. WILSON'S FANCY HORNPIPE. *Composed by* WM. FINDLAY, Haywood.

THE THISTLE HORNPIPE. *Composed by* WM. FINDLAY, Haywood.

THE BALL HORNPIPE. *Composed by* WM. FINDLAY, Haywood.

∨ Up Bow.　⊓ Down Bow.　⌣ Two Up or Down Bows.

KÖHLERS' "VIOLIN REPOSITORY," 11 NORTH BRIDGE, EDINBURGH.

MRS. FINDLAY'S, OF HAYWOOD, STRATHSPEY.

Composed by WILLIAM FINDLAY, Haywood.

Segue Reel.

MRS. FINDLAY'S, OF HAYWOOD, REEL. By WM. FINDLAY, Haywood.

Fine.

KILWINNING ARCHERS' STRATHSPEY.

Segue Reel. D.C.

∨ Up Bow.   ⊓ Down Bow.   ⌐⌐ Two Up or Down Bows.
KÖHLERS' "VIOLIN REPOSITORY," 11 NORTH BRIDGE, EDINBURGH,

THE RANDY WIVES OF GREENLAW REEL.

Fine.

J. TURNBULL'S COMPLIMENTS TO J. MANSON STRATHSPEY.

Segue Reel. D.C.

MARMONT'S REEL.

Fine.

∨ Up Bow.　⊓ Down Bow.　⌐•⌐• Two Up or Down Bows.

KÜHLERS' "VIOLIN REPOSITORY," 11 NORTH BRIDGE, EDINBURGH.

1.

THE CHORUS LANCERS QUADRILLES.

Newly out.

Arranged by W. Crow, Edinburgh.

2.

3.

Ritard.

∨ Up Bow.   ⌐ Down Bow.   ⁚—⁚ Two Up or Down Bows.

KÖHLERS' "VIOLIN REPOSITORY," 11 NORTH BRIDGE, EDINBURGH.

Fifth figure, *Staccato*—with Heel of Bow.

∨ Up Bow.   ⊓ Down Bow.   ∙——∙ Two Up or Down Bows.

PUBLISHED BY E. KÖHLER & SON, 11 NORTH BRIDGE, EDINBURGH.

Newly out. **THE MASHER POLKA.** *Composed by* W. B. Laybourn, 1885.

RAINBOW; OR, MIDNIGHT SCHOTTISCHE.

1st time.   2nd time.

(To be Continued.)

∨ Up Bow.   ⊓ Down Bow.   ⁑——⁑ Two Up or Down Bows.

Köhlers' "Violin Repository," 11 North Bridge, Edinburgh.

1. LA ENFANT VALSE. *Composed by* Miss M. LAYDOURN, Edinburgh, 1885.
Bowing and Fingering arranged by W. B. LAYBOURN.

RONDO, OR APE SHENKIN—Irish Air.

Allegretto.

Fine.

∨ Up Bow. ⊓ Down Bow. ⸳—⸳ Two Up or Down Bows.
PUBLISHED BY E. KÖHLER & SON, 11 NORTH BRIDGE, EDINBURGH.

RONDO—*Continued.*

Minor.

V Up Bow.   ⊓ Down Bow.   ⠄⠄ Two Up or Down Bows.

KÖHLERS' "VIOLIN REPOSITORY," 11 NORTH BRIDGE, EDINBURGH.

NEIL GOW'S RECOVERY STRATHSPEY.

Segue Reel. D.C.

MR. HAMILTON'S, OF WISHAW, REEL.

Fine. D.C.

LADY ELIZABETH LINDSAY'S STRATHSPEY.

Segue Reel. D.C.

∨ Up Bow. ⌐ Down Bow. •——•. Two Up or Down Bows.
KUHLEUS' "VIOLIN REPOSITORY," 11 NORTH BRIDGE, EDINBURGH.

LADY SUTHERLAND'S REEL.

Fine. D.C.

THE BRAES OF TULLYMET STRATHSPEY.

Segue Reel. D.C.

SIR RONALD M'DONALD'S REEL.

Fine. D.C.

∨ Up Bow.   ⊓ Down Bow.   ⌣ ⌣ Two Up or Down Bows.
KÖHLERS' "VIOLIN REPOSITORY," 11 NORTH BRIDGE, EDINBURGH.

MISS BAKER'S HORNPIPE.

THE ROCKET HORNPIPE.

WEST'S HORNPIPE.

∨ Up Bow.   ⊓ Down Bow.   _·___·_ Two Up or Down Bows.

Published by E. Köhler & Son, 11 North Bridge, Edinburgh.

THE NAVAL BRIGADE HORNPIPE. Composed by W. B. LAYBOURN, 1885.

PIRATES' HORNPIPE.

SANDERSON'S HORNPIPE. Composed by W. B. LAYBOURN, 1885.

∨ Up Bow.   ⊓ Down Bow.   ⌐·───·─ Two Up or Down Bows.

PUBLISHED BY E. KÖHLER & SON, 11 NORTH BRIDGE, EDINBURGH.

THE VIENNA POLKA.

LA GITANA POLKA.

OPERA POLKA.

(To be Continued.)

∨ Up Bow.　　⊓ Down Bow.　　⌣ Two Up or Down Bows.

KÜHLERS' "VIOLIN REPOSITORY," 11 NORTH BRIDGE, EDINBURGH.

Allegretto. **O DEAR WHAT CAN THE MATTER BE?—Variations.**

Bowing and Fingering arranged by W. B. LAYBOURN.

THE BELL POLKA. By E. Ames Muirpark, Dalkeith.

SANDY M'GAFF—Jig.

∨ Up Bow.   ⊓ Down Bow.   ⌣ Two Up or Down Bows.

Köhlers' "Violin Repository," 11 North Bridge, Edinburgh.

THE MARIE VALSES. *Composed by* J. MACKENZIE, Edin.

COMMON SCHOTTISCHE (Dewdrop).

TRIO.

D.C.

D.C.

IRISH JIG. *By* JOHN B. EASTON, *Edinburgh.*

∨ Up Bow. ⊓ Down Bow. ⌐—⌐ Two Up or Down Bows.

KÖHLERS' "VIOLIN REPOSITORY," 11 NORTH BRIDGE, EDINBURGH.

THE HUNTER'S VALSE.

1.

2.

Fine.

3.

1st. | 2nd. *D.C.*

v Up Bow.   ⌐ Down Bow.   •———•. Two Up or Down Bows.

KÖHLERS' "VIOLIN REPOSITORY," 11 NORTH BRIDGE, EDINBURGH.

VIOLIN PRIMO. **DUET FOR TWO VIOLINS.** *By* ROBERT BAILLIE.

VIOLIN SECONDO. **DUET FOR TWO VIOLINS.** *By* ROBERT BAILLIE.

∨ Up Bow. ⊓ Down Bow. ⸳——⸳ Two Up or Down Bows.

KÖHLERS' "VIOLIN REPOSITORY," 11 NORTH BRIDGE, EDINBURGH.

THE FIRTH HOUSE HORNPIPE. *Com. by* G. DUNCAN, Esq.

OLD WOODHOUSELEE CASTLE (Strathspey). *Com. by* G. DUNCAN, Esq.

Segue Reel. Volti Subito. D.C.

OLD WOODHOUSELEE REEL. *Com. by* G. DUNCAN, Esq.

D.C.

ᐯ Up Bow. ⊓ Down Bow. ⁓ Two Up or Down Bows.
KÖHLERS' "VIOLIN REPOSITORY," 11 NORTH BRIDGE, EDINBURGH.

THE STRANGER HORNPIPE.

THE PILGRIM HORNPIPE.

HOOLEY'S HORNPIPE.

Com. by R. M. HOOLEY.

(To be Continued.)

D.C.

V Up Bow. ⊓ Down Bow. ˌ——ˌ Two Up or Down Bows.

KÖHLERS' "VIOLIN REPOSITORY," 11 NORTH BRIDGE, EDINBURGH.

KÖHLERS' VIOLIN REPOSITORY.

No. 35.] PRICE 4D. [COPYRIGHT.

1. ## PRINCESS BEATRICE WALTZES.

Composed by WILLIAM FINDLAY, Broxburn.

Bowing and Fingering arranged by W. B. LAYBOURN.

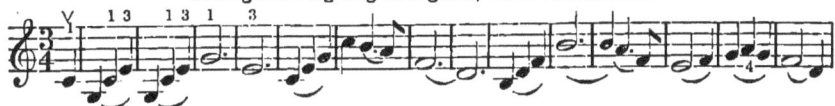

2.

Continued.

∨ Up Bow. ⊓ Down Bow. ‿⁚‿ Two Up or Down Bows.

3. **PRINCESS BEATRICE WALTZES—Continued.**

MISS ANDERSON'S POLKA. *By* Mackenzie.

THE A1 JIG. *By* Wm. Findlay, Broxburn.

∨ Up Bow. ⊓ Down Bow. •——• Two Up or Down Bows.
Köhlers' "Violin Repository," 11 North Bridge, Edinburgh.

HAWTHORNDEN. *Composed by* J. NASH, Dalkeith.

GENERAL GORDON'S HORNPIPE. *By* W. FINDLAY, Broxburn.

BLINKIN' TIBBIE—Hornpipe. *By* R. BAILLIE.

∨ Up Bow. ⊓ Down Bow. ⸱—⸱ Two Up or Down Bows.

Published by E. KÖHLER & SON, 11 North Bridge, Edinburgh.

WINCHBURGH CASTLE—Strathspey. *By* Wм. Findlay, Broxburn.

MISS BAIGRIE—Strathspey. *By* Peter Baillie.

MISS BAIGRIE—Reel. *By* Robert Baillie.

∨ Up Bow. ⊓ Down Bow. ⌣ Two Up or Down Bows.

KÖHLERS' "VIOLIN REPOSITORY," 11 NORTH BRIDGE, EDINBURGH.

277

THE OLD TOON OF BROXBURN REEL. *By* Wm. Findlay.

WHEN YOU GO TO THE HILL TAKE YOUR GUN—Strathspey.

D.C.

Segue Reel.

SCOTIA'S REEL. *Composed by* W. B. Laybourn.

D.C.

∨ Up Bow.   ⊓ Down Bow.   Two Up or Down Bows.
Köhlers' "Violin Repository," 11 North Bridge, Edinburgh.

DUET FOR TWO VIOLINS.

Violin Primo.

Allo. M. 120.

By Robert Baillie.

V Up Bow. ⊓ Down Bow. ∙───∙ Two Up or Down Bows.

Köhlers' "Violin Repository," 11 North Bridge, Edinburgh.

DUET FOR TWO VIOLINS.

VIOLIN SECUNDO.
Allo. M. 120.

By ROBERT BAILLIE.

∨ Up Bow.   ⊓ Down Bow.   ⌐‿⌐ Two Up or Down Bows.

D.C.

Published by E. KÖHLER & SON, 11 North Bridge, Edinburgh.

PRINCESS BEATRICE GALOP. *Com. by* W. B. LAYBOURN, 1885.

LITTLE JIM'S HORNPIPE.

(To be Continued.)

∨ Up Bow. ⊓ Down Bow. ⌣ ⌣ Two Up or Down Bows.

KÖHLERS' "VIOLIN REPOSITORY," 11 NORTH BRIDGE, EDINBURGH.

No. 36.] PRICE 4D.· [COPYRIGHT.

THE KEEL ROW—with Variations.

Bowing and Fingering arranged by W. B. LAYBOURN.

1ST VAR.

Fine.

∨ Up Bow. ⌐ Down Bow. ⌐ Two Up or Down Bows.

Published by E. KÖHLER & SON, 11 North Bridge, Edinburgh.

1. ## PRIDE OF THE NORTH QUADRILLE, *By* W. C. PATON.

∨ Up Bow.　⊓ Down Bow.　━ ━ Two Up or Down Bows.

3. PRIDE OF THE NORTH—Continued.

4.

V Up Bow. ⊓ Down Bow. ⌣ Two Up or Down Bows.
KÜHLERS' "VIOLIN REPOSITORY," 11 NORTH BRIDGE, EDINBURGH.

5. PRIDE OF THE NORTH—Continued.

Finale.

D.C.

∨ Up Bow.   ⊓ Down Bow.   •——• Two Up or Down Bows.
KÜHLERS' "VIOLIN REPOSITORY," 11 NORTH BRIDGE, EDINBURGH.

ARTHUR'S SEAT WALTZ.

1.

2nd time, 8va.

Louis J. Collins, Edinburgh.

VIOLIN PRIMO. **EXERCISE—"LODER."** *Arranged by* W. B. LAYBOURN.

VIOLIN PRIMO. **EXERCISE—"LODER."** *Arranged by* W. B. LAYBOURN.

ᴠ Up Bow. ⊓ Down Bow. Two Up or Down Bows.
Published by E. KÖHLER & SON, 11 North Bridge, Edinburgh.

VIOLIN SECUNDO. **EXERCISE—"LODER."** *Arranged by* W. B. LAYBOURN.

Andante.

VIOLIN SECUNDO. **EXERCISE—"LODER."** *Arranged by* W. B. LAYBOURN.

Andante.

V Up Bow. ⊓ Down Bow. Two Up or Down Bows.
KÖHLERS' "VIOLIN REPOSITORY," 11 NORTH BRIDGE, EDINBURGH.

CAPER FEY REEL.

D.C.

MASTER ERSKINE'S HORNPIPE.

By Neil Gow.

CALEDONIA'S WAIL FOR NEIL GOW STRATHSPEY.

2-3-4-3-2-1-3-2

2-3-4-3-2-1-4-1-2-3-4

1 2 3 4 3 1

D.C.

(To be Continued.)

v Up Bow.   ⊓ Down Bow.   ⁔ Two Up or Down Bows.

Published by E. Köhler & Son, 11 North Bridge, Edinburgh.

MUSICAL TREASURY.

Published by ERNEST KÖHLER & SON, II North Bridge, Edinburgh.

YEARLY, Post Free, 2s. 6d.

1885.

JUNE.—No. 73.   SECULAR.   MONTHLY, Price 2d.

IMPORTANT TO ALL TEACHERS OF SINGING!!

The Simplest and Easiest Method of learning to Sing at Sight from the Staff, is by means of the LETTER-NOTE SYSTEM, combining the advantages of the TONIC SOL-FA with the acknowledged Superiority of the OLD NOTATION.

Key E. Round for 4 voices.

Health, hap - pi - ness, plea - sure, Peace, joy with-out mea - sure,

Good for-tune and trea - sure,— All be thine!

EDUCATIONAL WORKS FOR PRIVATE SCHOOLS, CHOIRS, AND EVENING CLASSES.

ELEMENTARY SINGING MASTER, by DAVID COLVILLE. A Complete Course of Instruction on the Method. Eighty pp., cloth, 1s. 6d.; paper, 1s. In this course the notes are gradually withdrawn, training the pupils to dispense with their aid.

ELEMENTARY SINGING SCHOOL. Being the Exercises in the above work, published separately, for use of pupils, in 2 parts. 3d. each, in wrapper.

A GRADUATED COURSE of Elementary Instruction in Singing, by DAVID COLVILLE and GEORGE BENTLEY. In this course the Sol-fa initials are gradually withdrawn. In cloth, 1s. 6d.; in wrapper, 1s.

THE PUPIL'S HANDBOOK, containing the Songs, Exercises, &c., in the above course, published separately. In 2 parts, 3d. each.

In the following Courses the Notes are Lettered throughout :—

LETTER-NOTE SINGING METHOD. A course of Elementary Instruction in Singing arranged principally in Four-Part Harmony. Cloth, 1s. 6d.; paper, 1s.

CHORAL GUIDE. Being the Exercises of the above work, published separately in 2 parts, price 3d. each, in wrapper. This is a systematic elementary course, leading the Student by easy stages to a conversance with the art of singing.

THE CHORAL PRIMER. A Course of Elementary Training, by DAVID COLVILLE. 48 pp. in wrapper, price 6d.; or in six 8-page Nos., 1d. each; contains a more thorough and complete course of training than any other work published at the price.

SCHOOL MUSIC. Revised and enlarged edition. Part I., 32 pp., stitched in paper cover, price 3d., containing a complete course for Junior Pupils, with the addition of Voice-training Exercises and Elementary Instruction in the Theory of Music. The above is also published in eight halfpenny numbers of 4 pp. each. This is without exception the cheapest and most systematic educational work ever published.

THE JUNIOR COURSE. A Course of Elementary Practice in Singing, by DAVID COLVILLE. Arranged for two trebles, with ad lib. bass. In 6 penny numbers.

LETTER-NOTE VOCALIST. For Class and Home Singing, being a carefully chosen selection of favourite high-class Melodies, arranged as Duets and Trios; price, stitched in paper cover, 3d. each. Twelve Numbers already published.

DUETS.

No. 1. Ring for Christmas—*Scotch Air.*
     Home Again—*M. T. Pike.*
„ 2. Cherry Ripe—*C. E. Horn.*
„ 3. Love's Messenger—*Handel.*
„ 5. Won't you buy my Pretty Flowers? *Freedom's Land.*
„ 6. Say a kind word when you can—*J. R. Thomas.* Windows to the Sunrise—*G. F. Root.*
„ 8. Before all Lands—*Michael Kelly.* God Speed the Right—*German.* Our Country; our Fatherland—*Nageli.*
„ 9. Harvest Song—*Storace.* Dulce Domum—*Old Melody.* Holiday—*Nageli.*

TRIOS.

No. 4. The Bells, *arranged by G. Merritt, O.T.S.C.* Never say " I can't "—*W. B. Bradbury.*
„ 7. See our oars—*Sir John Stevenson.* How lovely are the Woods, *arranged by G. Merritt, O.T.S.C.*
„ 10. The Wild Rose—*Hauptman.* When Stormy Clouds—*Zumsteeg.* Don't Fret—*G. F. Root.*
„ 11. Have you ever heard the Echoes, *arr. by G. Merritt, O.T.S.C.*
„ 12. Where art thou Beam of Light?—*Sir H. R. Bishop*

THE ENTIRE TWELVE NUMBERS HANDSOMELY BOUND IN ONE VOLUME, CLOTH GILT, RED EDGES, PRICE 4s.

EASY CANTATAS, S.A.T.B., with Solos, &c., printed in Letter-note. Pilgrims of Ocean, 4d.; Maypole, 3d.

For Government, National, and Board Schools.

IMPORTANT TO SCHOOLMASTERS AND OTHERS.

The Letter-Note Method has obtained Government recognition, and Letter-Note pupils are entitled to have the Sol-fa initials appended to the sight-singing test supplied by the School Inspector.

SCHOOL MUSIC.—A cheap edition of the above, printed on inferior paper, containing Nos. I. to VI., stitched in wrapper, for the use of Government, Board, and National Schools, 24 pp., price 3d.

THE CODE SINGER, in 14 numbers, 8 pp. each, price 1d. Embracing all the requirements of the New Code for Divisions I., II., III., and IV. Divisions I. and II., in three numbers each. Divisions III. and IV., in four numbers each.

LETTER-NOTE VOCALIST. A selection of favourite Melodies, arranged as Duets and Trios. 4 pp., full music size. Twelve numbers already published; price 12s. 6d. per 100, assorted, if required; or 1s. 9d. per dozen.

LONDON : J. ADLEY & CO., Letter-Note Publishers, 26 Cornwall Road, Finsbury Park, N.

F. PITMAN, 20 Paternoster Row, E.C.

EDINBURGH : E. KOHLER & SON, 11 North Bridge; JOHN MENZIES & CO., 12 Hanover St.: JOHNSTONE & HUNTER, 4 Melbourne Pl.

GLASGOW: JOHN MENZIES & CO., 21 Drury Street; MORISON BROTHERS, Buchanan Street.

KINDER SPIEL:

OLD FRIENDS WITH NEW FACES;

A MUSICAL SKETCH FOR JUVENILES.

SOLO & CHORUS.

By J. C. GRIEVE.

An entirely original conception. Interesting to read; delightful to sing; amusing to perform; easy to get up.
Part I., see "Star" for July.   Old Notation in preparation and will shortly be issued.

We have every confidence in recommending this work to our readers; and, as both words and music are of special importance and interest, we respectfully request that our subscribers will recommend it to the notice of their friends.

ERNEST KOHLER & SON, 11 NORTH BRIDGE, EDINBURGH.

THE LEA RIG.

THE ATTENTION OF VOCALISTS IS CALLED TO REID'S ARRANGEMENT OF THIS ADMIRED SCOTTISH BALLAD. REMARKABLE ALIKE FOR SIMPLICITY AND EXQUISITE MELODY, IT IS RECEIVED WITH ENTHUSIASM WHEREVER IT IS SUNG.

"With a few masterly and skilful touches, Mr. Reid has transformed the original setting of 'THE LEA RIG' into a beautiful and refined Song, possessing all the characteristic charm of the finest Scotch Melodies."—*Review.*

Excerpt from Concert notice :—"Perhaps the most enjoyable number in the programme was the singing of 'THE LEA RIG' by a young lady, whose sympathetic voice and finished method could not have been heard to better advantage than in this lovely Scotch Ballad."

COMPASS E TO F.   ORDER EVERYWHERE.   PRICE 6D.

E. KOHLER & SON, 11 NORTH BRIDGE, EDINBURGH.

Musical Notes.

EDINBURGH.

THE Parkside Institute Choir gave an evening concert on Friday, 1st May, in the Oddfellows' Hall. The rendering of the choral numbers was only moderately good, the best efforts being "Wae's me for Prince Charlie," and Kuyvett's "The Bells of St. Michael's Tower." Miss Bannerman's singing was pleasing, especially in Behrend's pretty little song, "Auntie," and Miss Cowan showed some signs of culture in her delivery of Pinsuti's "All Hallow E'en." Mr. Stewart's fine voice was heard to advantage in "Sailing," but the young gentleman who sang "Bird of the Wilderness" has yet much to learn before he can give adequate expression to such compositions. Mr. James Dowie conducted, and Miss Henderson was the accompanist. A somewhat meagre audience received the various pieces of the programme with hearty applause.

THE Second Annual Concert, in aid of the Magazine Fund of Fountainbridge E.U. Church, took place in the hall of the chapel on Thursday evening, April 30. The programme was very well carried through, and, though not large, the audience was appreciative.

EDINBURGH CHORAL UNION. — The annual general business meeting of the Union was held on the 6th ult. in Dowell's Rooms, George Street—Mr. George Yule, president, in the chair—when the secretary's, treasurer's, and librarian's reports were submitted and approved. The following directors for the ensuing season were elected:—Hon. president, Sir H. Oakeley, Mus. Doc.; president, Mr. George Yule, F.E.I.S.; vice-president, Mr. James Waddel; secretary, Mr. Ralph Marshall; treasurer, Mr. D. S. Lunan; librarian, Mr. J. C. Porter; ladies' convener, Mr. John Sturrock; convener of Stewards, Mr. George Drysdale; committee, Messrs. J. T. Robertson, J. R. Craig, W. Mackay, and F. Paterson.

MR. THOMAS RICHARDSON, organist of St. Peter's Church, assisted by professional and amateur friends, gave an enjoyable evening concert in the Literary Institute on 7th May. The part-songs most efficiently rendered were, "The Dawn of Day" and "The Vikings," the interpretation of Mr. Richardson's glee, "How Calm, How Beautiful," not being conspicuously brilliant. Herr Gallrein and Mr. James Winram played delightful solos on violoncello and violin respectively, and Mr. Richardson himself was a tasteful accompanist. Master Willie Richardson's solo "Tell me, my Heart" (Bishop), Mr. J. Munro's "Let me love thee," Miss Mackenzie's "La Serenata," and Mr. Kirkhope's "I love thee," had the heartiest reception.

The Annual Recital of Stockbridge Free Church Musical Association took place in the church on Friday evening, 8th May. Under the baton of Mr. David Taylor, Dr. Stainer's cantata, "The Daughter of Jairus," and a few miscellaneous pieces were sung with excellent taste. Miss Wishart, Messrs. Taylor and Urquhart, on whom the solo parts in the cantata devolved, interpreted their individual pieces admirably. Of the miscellaneous pieces, perhaps the best rendered were, "O, Saviour of the World," "Peace, Perfect Peace," "The Beauteous Song," and "There is a Green Hill." Mr. John Hartley accompanied in his usual efficient manner. Mr. David Taylor conducted with marked ability and success. The church was comfortably filled with an appreciative audience.

A CONCERT of Sacred Music was given in Rosehall Church, Dalkeith Road, on April 29th, by the members of the congregational choir. There was a fairly large and very appreciative audience. The principal item in the programme was A. R. Gaul's sacred cantata, "The Holy City," which was very successfully rendered, the chorus being very good, the members singing with a decision and expression that indicated careful rehearsal. The miscellaneous part consisted of a new anthem, by the conductor, and several solos, which were all well rendered. Mr. Osborne W. Pinck was the conductor and organist.

GLASGOW.

THE musical association connected with Free St. Matthew's Church gave their annual concert in the

Berkeley Halls on the 6th ult., before a crowded audience. The Rev. C. A. Salmond, M.A., presided, and the first half of the programme comprised sacred solos, quartettes, part-songs, and choruses; whilst Haydn's "Spring" occupied the entire second half. "The heavens are telling," brought out the excellent tone of the association, although the attack was a little faulty. The prayer from "Mose in Egitto," "To Thee, Great Lord," displayed careful training; and Sullivan's "Watchman, what of the night?" was also well sung. The lady who sang Gounod's "The King of Love my Shepherd is" is possessed of a good voice, which will improve with further cultivation; and special mention must also be made of the young tenor who was deservedly encored for a thoroughly sympathetic rendering of the same composer's "Guardian Angel." Kreutzer's "Chapel," in quartette form, was fairly given, and Haydn's "Spring" was very creditably performed. At times the *tempo* was a little hurried, and this was particularly noticeable in the bass solo, "With joy the impatient husbandman," but the skilful way in which the accompaniment was handled prevented any evil effects. "Be propitious, bounteous Heaven," was fairly rendered, but, as usual with most choirs, the B flat in both trio and chorus was beyond the reach of all but one or two voices. On the whole, the concert reflected great credit on the painstaking and popular conductor, Mr. W. H. Murray. Mr. Hopper did ample justice to the pianoforte accompaniments.

On the 12th ult., in the Queen's Rooms, a fairy cantata, by Mr. Arthur J. Waley, a gentleman resident in Glasgow, was produced for the first time. The audience was a large one, composed mostly of ladies. Neither in text nor music does the cantata claim to be one of an advanced style; but it is, nevertheless, an attractive and sparkling little work. Mr. C. H. Wolnoth conducted with his wonted care and judgment, while the chorus of ladies made "the welkin ring" tunefully, and with good effect. The principal soloist (Mrs. Buntine) sustained the part of *Dame Hulda* gracefully and with artistic finish. Miss Jones displayed an excellent mezzo-soprano voice, and sang her music admirably. Miss Clark and also the tenor (Mr. Wareham) who forms the "bone of contention" among the ladies, deserve a word of commendation. The accompaniments, under the care of the composer himself, formed a most enjoyable feature of the performance.

It is stated that as Mr. A. C. Mackenzie, our Scottish musical composer, has left his Italian home to reside in this country, he will probably conduct the interpretation of "The Rose of Sharon" in the ensuing choro-orchestral season in the city.

An entertainment in connection with the music class of the Pollokshields Free Church was given on the 28th April. The concert was a fitting termination to a course of lessons given by Mr. M'Coll during the winter and spring months. Considering the fact that a large proportion of the members of the class were very young, the performance was in every way creditable alike to the class and their energetic and persevering conductor. Further, this fact must also be taken into account, that, amongst the residents in this fashionable suburb, singing from sol-fa is looked upon with very apparent prejudice, and that from amongst such families, as were represented on the platform, Mr. M'Coll could draw over 150 members, shows that even here sol-fa is at last being discovered as a valuable and trustworthy means of obtaining a real knowledge of music. Mr. M'Coll deserves very warm congratulation for the elaborate arrangements made and the entire success of this his first experiment in

this locality. The singing throughout was marked by taste and intelligence, and was warmly appreciated by the large audience which crowded the church. The soloists sang with care and expression, and the Misses White proved themselves to be very trustworthy accompanists. Several readings by Mr. Vallance were thoroughly enjoyed and heartily applauded.

The regretted death is announced, under mysterious circumstances, of Mr. Channon Cornwall, whose body was found in the Forth and Clyde Canal, Glasgow. He was missed on May 4th, and on May 6th his hat was found in the canal. Men were employed all Wednesday and Thursday, May 6th and 7th, searching for the body, and it was recovered by means of grappling-irons. Mr. Cornwall, who resided at Hillhead, Glasgow, was forty years of age, and known throughout the country as an organist of distinction. He received his early musical education, it is said, from his father, who has been for many years connected with Queenwood College. As he grew into manhood he came to Southampton, and, studying under Mr. Sharpe, secured in succession the organistship of Shirley Church and (in competition) of Romsey Abbey. Here he remained several years, moving hence to Alloa, in Scotland, some twelve or fifteen years ago, where he at once came to the front, and thence removed to Glasgow. His talents, which extended to original compositions and variations on popular airs, often selected by the celebrated Lambeth choir (from the name of their conductor) in their visits to Balmoral and their appearance in various places in Scotland, led to his making a wide acquaintance with the musical profession in the busy port of the North. He frequently "deputised" for Dr. Peace at the Cathedral, and for Mr. Lambeth at his church; and at the *monstre* popular concerts in St. Andrew's Hall. Though somewhat eccentric in manner, he was of a remarkably unpretentious and even retiring disposition; and, a cordial hater of shams, shoddy, and pretenders of all sorts, a very staunch and cordial personal friend. His untimely end will be most keenly regretted by those who knew him best, and could not fail to appreciate his talents and many good personal qualities. He was unmarried.

LEITH.

On April 30, a sacred concert was given by the members of Junction Road U.P. Church Musical Association, assisted by an amateur orchestra. The pieces performed were selections from "The Messiah," "Judas Maccabæus," "Samson," and "The Creation," and, taking into consideration the difficult nature of the works, the singers acquitted themselves creditably. The soloists—Miss Stein, Miss E. Ross, and Mr. Reid were in very good voice, but Mr. J. M. Graham has been heard to better advantage. The orchestra, under the leadership of Mr. D. Law, was at first rather disappointing, but they quite redeemed themselves later on by smooth and steady execution. Miss A. Sinclair and Mr. A. Sutherland presided at the piano and harmonium respectively, and the result of Mr. J. Burns' command of his forces was of a very satisfactory nature.

RINGFORD, KIRKCUDBRIGHT.

An Elementary Singing Class Concert was given in the hall here on the evening of Tuesday, the 28th ult., Mr. J. Welsh, Castle-Douglas, conductor. Among the sacred pieces sung were—"The Rescue" and "A Dream," for the first time introduced in the district; while, in the secular part, were such as "We ride the foaming sea,"

"A life on the ocean wave," "Ye Mariners of England," &c. Several solos, duets, and trios were also interspersed. The rendering of the whole programme was much appreciated by the audience. Mr. Hunter, teacher, Tongland Public School, moved a vote of thanks to Mr. Welsh and his class for the great musical treat provided, and expressed surprise at the state of perfection attained in so short a period of training. He also spoke in laudatory terms of the excellent purity of tone and attention to expression evinced throughout. This is the second annual concert given here by Mr. Welsh, who has established himself a favourite in the district.

SCOTSMEN AND SCOTCH MUSIC.

THE following instance shows that Scotch music will make a Scotsman do anything when out of his own country :—A gentleman, who was a first-rate performer of Scotch music on the violin, spent a winter in Exeter, and of course soon became acquainted with the musical *dilettanti* of the place. Dining one day with a professor, the conversation turned upon Scotch music, and a strong argument arose as to its bearing competition with foreign music; the Scotsman, whom we shall for the present designate the fiddler, insisting that, when properly played, nothing could excel it—the professor on the other hand, insisting that it was only fit for the barn-yard. "I'll tell you what," says the fiddler, "I'll lay you a bet of five pounds, that if a party of Scotsmen can be got together, I'll make them shed tears one minute, sing the next, and dance the third." "Done," says the professor; "and if your music is capable of that, I will not only pay you the five pounds with pleasure, but will be convinced that it is the most enlivening, pathetic, and best music in the world." The difficulty arose as to getting an opportunity for a trial. But this was soon obviated by a third party informing them that a number of young Scotsmen dined annually at the Old London Hotel on the anniversary of Burns' birth-day. This was a capital opportunity for the fiddler; for these young men, being principally raw-boned, over-grown Scots lads who had recently left their own country to make their fortunes in the great metropolis, were the very ones upon whom he was sure to make a hit. All being now arranged, and the utmost secrecy being agreed upon, the eventful day was anxiously looked for. At length it came; and the fiddler and professor, by an introduction to one of the party, got an invitation to the dinner. There were twelve altogether sat down, and a right merry party they soon became, for the whisky toddy was not spared when the memory of any of Scotia's bards was proposed. The fiddler was not long in perceiving that he had got among a right musical set, and he waited patiently till they were in that happy state when they were fit for anything. At length he gave a wink to the professor, who at once proposed that his friend should favour them with a Scotch tune on the violin. "Capital! capital!" cried the whole party. The violin was brought, and all were in breathless anxiety. The fiddler chose for his first tune, "Here's a health to them that's awa'," and played it in the most solemn and pathetic manner. "That's a waefu' tune," said a great, big, raw-boned youth in his next neighbour. "It is that, Sandy; there's muckle in that tune, man. It reminds me o' ane that's gane;" Jamie at the same time giving a deep sigh, and drawing his hand over his long gaunt face to hide the tears which were trickling down his cheeks. The fiddler with his keen eye soon perceived that before he got through the second part of the tune he would have them all in the same mood. He therefore threw his whole soul into the instrument, played the tune as he had never done before; and as the last four bars of the tune died away like the distant echo, there was not a dry cheek amongst the company. Now is the time, thought the fiddler; and, without stopping a moment, struck up, in a bold, vigorous style, "Willie brew'd a peck o' maut." Out went the handkerchiefs, away went the tears. "Chorus!" cried the fiddler; and in an instant all struck up—

> "For we are na fou we're nae that fou,
> But just a drappie in our e'e;
> The cock may craw, the day may daw,
> But aye we'll taste the barley bree!"

The song ended, up struck the fiddler, in his best style, the reel of "Jenny dang the weaver." "Hey, ye devils!" cried Sandy. "Scotland for ever!" cried Jamie; and in an instant tables, chairs, and glasses, were scattered in all directions, and the whole party dancing and jumping like madmen. Out ran the affrighted professor (for he did not know what might come next); up came the landlady with her terrified train of inmates. But none durst enter the room, the hurras and thumps on the floor being so boisterous; and it was only upon the entry of a Scots traveller, who had just arrived, and who cried to the fiddler for any sake to stop, that order was restored. It is needless to say that the professor paid his bet cheerfully, and was fully convinced of the effect of Scotch music when properly played; and that the landlady took care that the fiddler never came into her house again on Burns's anniversary dinner.

PAGANINI.

(Continued from last month.)

PAGANINI's playing made an extraordinary impression on Liszt, who was twenty years of age when the great violinist took Paris by storm. It is generally admitted that Paganini's violin capriccios and wondrously expanded art of violin-playing gave Liszt the impulse towards the treatment of the pianoforte which resulted in the creation of a new school of pianists. Liszt was in London when news of Paganini's death reached him, and the following essay may be taken as his tribute laid upon the fresh grave of Paganini, the artist. It has also the strongest interest as self-expression :—

*   *   *   *

The flame of Paganini's life is extinguished, and with it one of those mighty breathings of Nature for which she appears to rouse herself only to reinspire it immediately. With it has vanished a marvellous apparition, such as the whole compass of art has seen but once—this great and marvellous occasion.

The height of this unsurpassable and unattainable genius excludes all imitation. No one will ever tread in his footsteps; no fame stands on equal ground beside his reputation; his name will be breathed without a compeer. Where is there an artist life which, in so high a degree, can point to so shadowless a sunshine of glory, to so kingly a name accorded him by universal judgment, to so infinite a chasm as that which the verdict of mankind has opened between him and all competitors?

When Paganini, already forty years old, came before the public with a talent that had reached the highest point of all attainable perfection, the world wondered at him as at a supernatural appearance. The sensation which he excited was so tempestuous, his power over the imagination so mighty, that it could not be kept within the limits of reality. There arose tales of the sorcerer's art, and spectres of the middle ages. They sought to unite the wonders of his playing with the past; they would explain his inexplicable genius by inexplicable facts, and almost came to the conclusion that he had sold his soul to the evil one, and that the fourth string, from which he elicited such enchanting melodies, was the intestines of his wife, whom he had killed with his own hand.

He travelled through all Europe. The multitude, allured and enchanted by his playing, strewed gold at his feet, and sought to bestow the fairest reward on artists distinguishing themselves on their instruments by baptising them after his name. There were now Paganinis of the piano, of the counterbass, of the guitar. The violinists racked their brains to find out his secret. In the sweat of their brow they laboured through the difficulties which he had created in play, and with which they only extorted a pitying smile from the public, while they could not even enjoy the satisfaction of hearing their names mentioned in the world of art. Thus Paganini's ambition, if he possessed any, enjoyed the rare happiness of drinking in the air of unattainable heights, disturbed by no injustice, disquieted by no indifference. His sunset in the grave was not even darkened by the grievous shadow of an heir to his glory.

Who will believe it without having been a witness of the same? This talent to which the world gave so lavishly what it often denies to greatness—fame and riches; this man before whom they shouted so enthusiastically, passed by the multitude without associating with them. No one knew the sentiments which moved his heart; the golden ray of his life gilded no other existence; no communion of thought and feeling bound him to his brethren. He remained a stranger to every affection, to every passion, a stranger even to his own genius—for what is genius else than a priestly power, revealing God to the human mind; and Paganini's god has never been other than his own gloomy, mournful self.

I pronounce these severe words with inward reluctance. Does one blame the dead or praise the living—in both cases one must expect small thanks, I know. I am aware, too, that, under pretence of respecting the sanctity of the grave, in judging a man, the falsehood sometimes immediately follows the deceit of heresy, and that some deeds of benevolence will be quoted which appear to contradict such accusations. Yet, what are solitary cases against the testimony of a whole life? Consistent evil is as difficult in the actions of a man as consistent goodness. I ask, then, using the word egotism not so much in a narrow as in a comprehensive sense, and in reference to the artist rather than to the man—am I not authorised in describing the end and aim of Paganini as a narrow egotism?

Be that as it may, peace to his memory! He was great. All greatness bears its own justification. Do we know at what price a man buys his renown? Can the void which Paganini has left behind—can it be soon filled up? Are the main or incidental points to which he owed his supremacy, and which I joyfully accord him—are they of a kind to be renewed by repetition? Will the kingly, artistic dignity acquired by him pass into other hands? Is the artist king to be expected once again?

I say it without hesitation—no second Paganini will arise. The wonderful coincidence of a gigantic talent, with all the circumstances appropriate to his apotheosis, will appear in the history of art as a solitary instance. An artist who, in the present day, should strive intentionally to throw a cloak of mystery around himself in order to set minds in astonishment as Paganini did, would

cause no surprise, and—even supposing him to be possessed of inestimable talent—the remembrance of Paganini would accuse him of charlatanism and plagiarism. Moreover, the public of the present day requires other things of the artist whom it favours, and a similar glory and power can be won only by entirely opposite means.

To comprehend art—not as a convenient means for egotistical advantages and unfruitful celebrity, but as a sympathetic power, which unites and binds men together; to educate one's own life to that lofty dignity which floats before talent as an ideal; to open the understanding of artists to what they should and what they can do; to rule public opinion by the noble ascendency of a high, thoughtful life; and to kindle and nourish in the minds of men that enthusiasm for the beautiful which is so nearly allied to the good—that is the task which the artist has to set before him who feels himself strong enough to strive to be Paganini's heir.

This task is difficult, but not impossible of fulfilment. Broad paths are open to every endeavour, and a sympathetic recognition is assured to every one who consecrates his art to the divine service of a conviction—of a consciousness. We all foresee a transformation of our social positions. Without exaggerating the importance of the artist as regards them, without—as has already perhaps often been done—wishing to announce his mission in pompous expressions, an artist may, at least, have the firm conviction that to him also a place is destined in the plans of Providence, and that he, too, is called to be a fellow toiler in a new and noble work.

May the artist of the future with joyful heart renounce the vain and egotistic part, which, as we hope, has found its last brilliant representative in Paganini! May he set his aim *within*, and not without! and may virtuosoship be the means, and not the end! May he, moreover, never forget that, though it is said, *Noblesse oblige*, quite as much, and even more, *Génie oblige!*

THE STORY OF "AULD ROBIN GRAY."—This exquisite ballad was written by Lady Anne Lindsay, daughter of the fifth Earl of Balcarres. She was born on November 27, 1750, and at the early age of twenty-one produced the ballad which Sir Walter Scott says "is worth all the dialogues which Corydon and Phylis have had together, from the days of Theocritus downwards." In 1793, Lady A. Lindsay married Mr. Andrew Barnard, son of the Bishop of Limerick, with whom she went out to the Cape on his appointment as Colonial Secretary under Lord Macartney. Mr. Barnard dying at the Cape, his widow returned to London, where she enjoyed the friendship of Burke, Windham, and others, until her death, which occurred in the year 1825. It was not until she was in her seventy-third year that Lady Barnard made known the secret of the authorship of this ballad. An amusing story is told in connection with its production. On Lord Balcarres' estate was a shepherd of the name of Robin Gray, and for some act of his Lady Anne resolved to immortalise his memory. Upon her little sister entering her room one day, Lady Anne said, "I have been writing a ballad, my dear; and I am oppressing my heroine with many misfortunes. I have already sent her Jamie to sea, broken her father's arm, made her mother fall sick, and given her auld Robin Gray for a lover; but I wish to load her with a fifth sorrow in the four lines. Help me to one, I pray." "Steal the cow, sister Anne," said her sister. Accordingly, we are told that the cow was "lifted."—*From Cassell's "Illustrated British Ballads."*

AN INTERESTING STORY OF GEORGE II. AND THE DUCHESS OF QUEENSBERRY.

An anecdote is told of the Duchess of Queensberry's being forbid the Court, which belongs to the literary history of the cleverest opera in our own or any other language—Gay's famous production. Walpole justly regarded himself as caricatured in the "Beggar's Opera," obtained the Duke of Grafton's authority, as Lord Chamberlain, to suppress the representation of his next opera, "Polly." Gay resolved to publish it by subscription; and his patroness, the Duchess of Queensberry, put herself at the head of the undertaking, and solicited every person she met to subscribe. As the Duchess was handsome, a wit, and of the first fashion, she obtained guineas in all directions, even from those who dreaded to encourage this act of defiance. The Duchess' zeal, however, increased with her success; and she even came to the drawing-room, and, under the very eye of majesty, solicited subscriptions for an opera the Monarch had forbidden to be acted. When the King came into the drawing-room, seeing the Duchess very busy in a corner with three or four persons, he asked her what she was doing? She answered, "What was most agreeable, she was sure, to anybody so humane as his Majesty, for it was an act of charity; and a charity to which she did not despair of bringing his Majesty to contribute." This proceeding was so much resented, that Mr. Stanhope, the Vice-Chamberlain to the King, was sent in form to the Duchess to forbid her coming to Court. The message was verbal; but she desired to send a written answer—wrote it on the spot—and thus furnished a document, whose style certainly exhibited more sincerity than courtiership:—"That the Duchess of Queensberry is surprised and well pleased that the King has given her so agreeable a command as to stay away from Court, where she never came for diversion, but to bestow a great civility on the King and Queen. She hopes that, by such an unprecedented order as this, the King will see as few as he wishes at his Court, particularly such as dare to think or speak truth I dare not do otherwise, and ought not, nor could have imagined that it would not have been the very highest compliment I could possibly pay the King, to endeavour to support truth and innocence in his house—particularly when the King and Queen both told me that they had not read Mr. Gay's play. I have certainly done right, then, to stand by my own words rather than by his Grace of Grafton's, who had neither made use of truth, judgment, nor honour through this whole affair, either for himself or his friends.—C. QUEENSBERRY." When her Grace had finished this paper, drawn up, as Lord Harvey observes, "with more spirit than accuracy," Stanhope requested of her to think again, and give him a more courtly message to deliver. The Duchess took her pen, and wrote another; but it was so much more disrespectful than be asked for the former one, and delivered it. There was, of course, a prodigious quantity of court-gossip on this occasion; and, doubtless, though some pretended to be shocked, many more were amused at the dashing oddity of the Duchess. But public opinion, on the whole, blamed the Court. It certainly was infinitely childish in the King to have inquired into what the Duchess was doing among her acquaintances in the drawing-room; it was equally beneath the natural notions of royal dignity that the King should put himself in a state of hostility with a subject, and in so trifling a matter as the subscription to an unpublished opera; and it was equally impolitic, for the world was sure to range itself on the side of the woman, especially when that woman was handsome, eccentric, and rich. It produced some inconvenience, however, to the lady's husband, as he in consequence gave up the office of Admiral of Scotland.

THE REMAINS OF BEETHOVEN AND SCHUBERT.

The remains of Beethoven and Schubert were recently transferred from the burial ground of Waehring, one of the suburbs of Vienna, to the Central Friedhof, a large new cemetery just outside the town, where ground has been specially reserved for the interment of great men. This tardy tribute of honour to two great heroes of music will relieve many people's minds, for it has long been a source of amazement to those who have visited the graves at Waehring, that such meagre sepulchres should mark the last resting place of such men. The old graveyard of Waehring has been closed for the last seven years, and, as I saw it recently, it looked dirty and neglected beyond description. The tomb of Beethoven was erected more than four years ago; until then his remains had been left where they were deposited after his death, a common stone slab alone indicating the spot where they lay. This slab has been replaced by something better; and when the change was made his ashes were put into a metal coffin. The grave is now surrounded by a low iron railing, and at the foot stands a stone slab, pyramid-shaped, bearing for all inscription the name of Beethoven in large gilt letters. It is, however, still of modest appearance, and no stranger would think of looking there for the burial-place of Ludwig Van Beethoven. The tomb of Schubert is more pretentious, but, if possible, less imposing, and altogether unworthy of the great genius whose remains lie beneath.

A bronze bust, reproducing the features of the immortal tone-poet is placed at the upper extremity. But, though we know Schubert was not of prepossessing appearance, yet the metallic work of art I saw lacks that expression so admirably rendered in a portrait taken from life, which hangs, if I mistake not, in the reception hall of the Vienna Conservatoire. On the stone pediment behind the bust is the following inscription—"Musical art has buried here a rich possession, but still brighter hopes." Surely the memory of Franz Schubert might have inspired a nobler epitaph than that. When the transfer to the Central Friedhof was effected, a monument was provided for the tomb of Beethoven by the Society of the Conservatoire, and another for that of Schubert by the Vienna Maennergsangverein or Men's Choral Union.

IPHIGENIA IN AULIS.

Gluck's "Iphigenia in Aulis" proved the final overthrow of the Piccini faction which so fiercely contested the progress of the master reformer. Many strange stories are told concerning its first performance. It was in 1774, April 19. At midnight the opera drew to a close, and the opera house at Paris re-echoed with applause. "Iphigenia" had triumphed, and the excitement was intense. Tears flowed, smiles beamed around, sobs were audible, Gluck's name sounded from a thousand lips.

In one of the boxes sat the Queen—Marie Antoinette, in regal attire. Louis XVI. stood beside her, his face pale and in deep agitation.

"Oh God!" said he suddenly, "what if this flash of joy should be turned to glow of fury! what a picture!"

Marie Antoinette shuddered at the thought as she looked upon the easily influenced mass of people.

"Where is Gluck?" she asked in a whisper.

Soon the master was sent for. Entering, he bent low before the King. The Queen drew near, and with a smile pressed upon the composer's brow a green laurel wreath.

Gluck raised himself up, an uncertain gleam in his eyes; he passed his hand over his pale brow, and stared at the Queen with an expression of horror.

"Merciful heavens!" he cried, "what a fearful sight! Quick, my Queen, wipe away that terrible streak of blood which encircles your beautiful neck! Who gave you such an ornament?—destroy it! every instant the crimson stain widens! your fair head totters! the band is a stream! Too late! Oh! merciful heaven—" as he uttered this cry he sank into a swoon.

"Gluck must see spirits," whispered the King in a terrible whisper; "the excitement of his victory has unnerved him."

Marie Antoinette's whole frame shuddered, and sobbing like a frightened child, she tore off the costly necklace of rubies, which like a glistening band encircled her snowy neck. Then commending the still unconscious composer to a physician, leaning on the King's arm she tremblingly left the box.

* * * * *

Was it an inspiration that caused Gluck to utter those awful words? How could he know—that glorious Orpheus of the modern ages, that his prophetic vision had lifted the veil of the horrible future!

Nineteen years after the night on which "Iphigenia" triumphed, the crimson band which encircled the neck of the unhappy Queen became a stream indeed! In October, 1793, Marie Antoinette's head fell beneath the axe of the guillotine!—*Musical People.*

A VISIT TO THE LONDON CONSERVATOIRE OF MUSIC.

THIS very successful institution will be found in Porchester Square, Hyde Park. It is a large and handsome building, in a beautiful and healthy neighbourhood. It is out of the crowd, but conveniently placed within a few yards of the Royal Oak Railway Station. It stands alone, "untouched by baser stuff," partly surrounded with garden ground; and there is a fine view from almost every window.

I make my visit at about eleven in the morning, and find the page almost lost amongst a number of young ladies he has just admitted. These are students, ready for the morning work. Professors of the different branches of music make their appearance now and then, coming and going through the hall from different parts of the establishment, and the place is busy with greeting and hand-shaking.

Presently Mr. Lansdowne Cottell, the genial and enterprising director, makes his appearance. He leads the way through a running fire of morning salutations; and I leave the hall with him to have a quiet survey, while the students are making themselves ready, and finding their different class-rooms.

I am soon impressed with the fact that the place is comfortably and almost luxuriously furnished—and very clean. In any part of the building the feet find themselves comfortable on good carpets. As the Conservatoire is full of students who not only learn here but live here as boarders, these home advantages are doubly acceptable.

In every room there is an Ascherberg or an English piano of the best make. As far as I know there may be one in the kitchen also. I did not go to see, but it would not surprise me to find that even the cooks are allowed to refine the sauce with a little harmony, and plaice a sole amongst the fish. The French, German, and Italian professors on the establishment have my full permission to set this joke to music, or translate it into their own language.

The whole of the Conservatoire is fitted like a mansion, and there is throughout an air of comfort and prosperity. Mr. Cottell is successful and happy in his work, and "full of it" all the time. When he gets mentally tired, he takes his tricycle out of the stable and enjoys a breather to the seaside. He has trained many good singers for the public, and several are famous. And they have not forgotten him either. On a large sideboard, in one of the rooms, I noticed a massive silver épergne about four feet high, surrounded by four other large pieces of silver—a suitably-inscribed present from students who have remembered the good training and sensible advice received at his hands.

The work of the morning has commenced. I find each room with its class and professor at work, and it is time Mr. Cottell made a start, too. I accompany him to another part of the building to hear him give a singing lesson. In a large and pleasant room we find about fifteen or twenty young ladies awaiting his coming. Their chairs are arranged in a large semicircle, and they are sitting very much at home with plenty of gossip for mutual entertainment. "Now, ladies, standing if you please," and the next moment Mr. Cottell is at the piano, and the work has commenced. In the midst of striking chords and accompanying their songs, he is continually illustrating, advising, encouraging, or correcting bad productions. The exercises and comments go merrily on together, until this preliminary part of the singing lesson is ended, and all are seated. Now, each pupil has to sing a song separately, with stops and comments as occasion may require. Shortcomings are promptly set right, and good points are quickly caught, encouraged, and developed. All is bright, and earnest, and interesting. Indeed, the instruction throughout is in every way made attractive, sensible, and diverting. My listening is brought to an end by the entrance of Mrs. Cottell, who, in her happy, business-like way, and with her hands full of letters, comes to have her word, and give her welcome. I must tell you that Mrs. Cottell knows the art side and the business side of every branch of the work, and is thus enabled to enter fully into the management and spirit of the undertaking.

The London Conservatoire of Music can boast of a complete orchestra and choir, the conductors being Dr. Hartmann and Mr. Walter Wesche. There are also elocution classes, and many more advantages than we have space to speak of. For many years students from the Conservatoire have distinguished themselves at the Monday and Popular Concerts, at Covent Garden, and with the Carl Rosa and D'Oyly Carte Opera Companies. This of itself will suggest that the system of tuition is of a thoroughly practical kind and leads to success. Indeed, managers write from all parts to thank the Conservatoire for new talent.

I advise all who are interested to send for a prospectus. By-the-bye, an extra series of concerts is announced for the season, concluding July 9, at St. James's Great Hall, when Mr. Sims Reeves, Herr Oberthür, and many other eminent artists will appear.—*The Age.*

Musical Treasury.

EDINBURGH, JUNE 1, 1885.

ADVERTISEMENTS.

Advertisements will be received at the following rate:—

One page,	.	.	.	£1 0 0
Half page,	.	.	.	0 11 0
Quarter page,	.	.	.	0 6 0
One-eighth page,	.	.	.	0 3 6
Three lines,	.	.	.	0 1 0

Advertisements must reach the *Treasury* Office not later
than the 20th of each month.

NOTICE.

All Advertisements appear in the "Musical Star" *and*
"Musical Treasury."

As both journals have a large and increasing circulation,
advertisers can hardly fail to appreciate the advantages
offered by the "Star" *and* "Treasury" *as advertising*
mediums, only one charge being made.

The "Musical Star" *and* "Musical Treasury" *may be*
obtained through all Booksellers and Newsagents, or from
the Office, 11 North Bridge, Edinburgh.

"A TASTE FOR MUSIC."

THOUGH Goldsmith was perhaps not the first to make
the discovery, he has certainly expressed most felicitously
the idea that the cultivation of taste makes no actual
addition to our happiness. We may imagine that when
we have studied the great masters, and are able to
appreciate the delicate beauties of their works, to talk
learnedly of this oratorio or that opera, we are the
possessors of an amount of happiness which the artisan
with his concertina can never know. But is there any
proof that it is so? Absolutely none! Indeed, the
proof is all the other way. We cannot imagine for a
moment that the workman who comes home, plays his
melodeon for several hours on end, and in the belief that
his musical instrument should not be shut in a box any
more than that a candle should be placed under a bushel,
parades the street and gives the public a share of his joys;
we cannot bring ourselves to think that he is doing this
merely to fill up his time before going to rest. The notion
is too ludicrous. He is enjoying himself most thoroughly.
The misguided individual, too, who has stored his memory
with songs, sentimental and tragical, is delighted with
himself when he trolls off a few of them to an admiring
circle in one of those dens where the atmosphere is
rendered unwholesome and sickening by reason of villanous
tobacco smoke and the fumes of stale beer. To him a
pianoforte solo by Dr. Charles Hallé, or a nocturne played
by Madame Norman Neruda, would be as destitute of
interest as a lecture on Kant's Metaphysics of Ethics.
We need not, however, cite the highest and the lowest
musical tastes as if the matter ended there. Between the
two there are innumerable shades and diversities which
may be roughly described as ascending from the keyed
flute, through the cheap harmonium and square piano, to
the better class of American and church organs. You
have acquaintances who will tell you that they are very
fond of music, "though they can't do anything at it
themselves." These worthy people take a curious method
of indicating their fondness, namely, by eagerly entering
into trivial conversation or staring out at the window,
while in response to their request you are performing the
choicest pieces in your repertoire. One may be excused
for thinking that these good people are under a delusion in
imagining they have a taste for music. There are many
whom to doubt would be the height of uncharitableness,
and the theory that they are under a delusion is therefore
at once the most reasonable and the most charitable. But
the people who perhaps deserve the greatest commiseration
are those who have absolutely no taste for music—who
have actually no music in their souls. The cases are
happily comparatively few, but we have met people who
did not know one tune from another. Perfect candour in
stating the fact is, however, a characteristic of this class,
and contrasts favourably with the conduct of those who
say they like music, and look as if they were on heckles
when they are listening to it! Let us note, however,
that cultivated musical perception has its disadvantages.
Supposing we go through a course of musical study by
which the ear is trained to perfect tune and time, it
naturally follows that any violations in these particulars
will be exceedingly annoying to us, and the annoyance
will be in proportion to the thoroughness of our training.
Everybody knows that this vexation frequently comes
upon us at the most inconvenient times. We wish
perhaps to enter into the spirit of the praise in public
worship, when a bass at the back drives the devotion out
of us by singing two notes behind time, or a thin tenor
hangs fire with his s s.f m at the end of the tune.
Though, as we indicated at the commencement, cultivated
musical taste may not yield us in the abstract greater
happiness than is enjoyed by the parties who troll
"Wait till the clouds," &c., &c., on the melodeon, do not
let us relinquish the pleasant task of adding to our musical
knowledge. Instead of being contented with the standard
which prevails, higher though that standard is undoubtedly
becoming, let us aid by every means in our power the
efforts which are being made all over Britain to popularise
the works of the really great composers.

MUSICAL LITERATURE.

THE CHILD'S VOICE. By Emil Behnke and Lennox Browne, F.R.C.S., Ed. London: Sampson, Low, Marston, Searle, and Rivington. Price, 3s. 6d.

THE appearance of this volume, which forms a valuable appendix to the well-known work "Voice, Song, and Speech," merits a cordial welcome, inasmuch as it is perhaps the only complete and reliable authority extant, bearing directly on the treatment and cultivation of the voice in children. Now that the teaching of singing plays so prominent a part in our schools, it is all the more desirable that the opinions of the most distinguished vocalists and voice-trainers, with regard to the conditions under which boys and girls may with safety begin a systematic course of voice culture, should be placed on record for the guidance and information of the many preceptors who are comparatively inexperienced. Apart, however, from its distinct educational value, " The Child's Voice" has a peculiar interest for parents, the majority of whom have probably hitherto never given the subject even a passing thought. The tendency to overstrain the juvenile organ wherever there is the slightest indication of precocity, and the disastrous results that almost invariably ensue when due care is not exercised during puberty, are brought out in an eminently practical manner. In brief, it may be said that "The Child's Voice" is a treatise that ought to be read, and carefully digested by all who are concerned and interested in the training of young vocalists.

New Music.

B. WILLIAMS, 19 Paternoster Row, London, E.C.

Little Love. Song. Words by G. Clifton Bingham. Music by Ciro Pinsuti. Price 2s. net.—*Trust and be True.* Song. Words by G. Clifton Bingham. Music by Ciro Pinsuti. Price 2s. net.—*All Hallow E'en.* Song. Words by Mary Mark Lemon. Music by Ciro Pinsuti. Price 2s. net. Few musicians understand the art of beautifying a simple melody with rich harmonic effects better than Signor Pinsuti, and in *Little Love* he is, in this respect, at his very best. It is a captivating little ballad, and worthy of all praise. Two settings—E flat and G; compass, B flat to D. *Trust and be True* is a capital song that will be most effective when rendered with expression by a baritone voice. Two settings—E flat and F; compass, B flat to E flat. *All Hallow E'en* is already so well known that we need only record our opinion that it is a pretty song with a catching waltz refrain. Three settings—E flat, F, and G; compass, B flat to E flat.—*Our Captain.* Song. Words by Edward Oxenford. Music by William M. Hutchison. Price 2s. net. While appreciating the difficulties of song writers in attempting to infuse anything like freshness into new sea songs, it must be acknowledged that rather more originality might reasonably have been looked for from the composer of *Ehren on the Rhine* than appears in this nautical ditty. It can hardly be said to rise above the commonplace, and only serves to remind us of older and, it must be admitted, better songs. Three settings—E flat, F, and G; compass, B flat to E flat.—*Who can say?* Song. Words by G. Clifton Bingham. Music by Frederic Mullen. Price 2s. net. An expressive and graceful love song, which would have been all the more attractive had the composer omitted the antiquated idea of a peal of bells. The bells fortunately do not extend over more than

a few bars, and apart from this it is a charming composition. Two settings—E flat and F; compass, C to E.—*Tête a Tête.* Polka. By Ambroise Leduc. Price 1s. 6d. net. A sprightly and tuneful dance measure. Very easy to play.—*Azalea.* Scottische. By Percy Lester. Price 1s. 6d. Although people are rather conservative in the matter of Schottische music, and, as a rule, prefer the old-fashioned tunes, *Azalea* is by no means deficient in merit, and is well worthy of favourable notice.—*Birdie's Nest.* Song. Words by M. Inglis Ball. Music by Odoardo Barri. Price 2s. net. A mother singing her baby to sleep is depicted in words and music that are beautiful and appropriate. The symphony and accompaniment are very quaint and pretty. Three settings—D, F, and A flat; compass, A to C.—*Some one.* Song. Words by Mary Mark Lemon. Music by H. Trotère. Price 2s. net. If a trifle conventional in its general construction, this ballad is certainly not devoid of artistic merit, and being easy both to sing and play, should win a fair measure of popularity. Two settings—F and A flat; compass, C to D.

H. BERESFORD, 99 New Street, Birmingham.

Beyond the Realms of Night. Song. Words by David Grayl. Music by Ciro Pinsuti. Price 2s. net. Signor Pinsuti has never been happier in his work than in this beautiful song. Expressively sung, it will be listened to with pleasure and attention, and should achieve more than an average amount of success. Three settings—D, F, and G; compass, B to D.

E. ASCHERBERG & Co., 211 Regent Street, London, W.

Nocturne in B flat. By G. J. Rubini. Price 2s.—*Militaria.* Fantasia. By Emil Leonardi. Price 2s.—*Le Réveillon, Air, Louis XV.* By G. J. Rubini. Price 2s. The above three pieces possess considerable merit, and are by no means difficult. The *Nocturne* is a smoothly written, graceful theme; while *Militaria* is always interesting, and at times brilliant. *Le Réveillon* will find many admirers, being an extremely quaint and pretty movement in the old style.—*The Primrose Badge.* Song. Words by Arthur Chapman. Music by Odoardo Barri. Price 2s. Among Conservatives this song ought to have a large sale. The words, if a trifle high falutin, are decidedly clever, and sing in praise of the late Lord Beaconsfield's statesmanship, and of toryism generally. The melody and harmony are admirable, and being most appropriate, the result, as a whole, is a really capital song. Key D; compass, D sharp to E.—*Life's Journey.* Song. Words by Lillie Davis. Music by D. M. Davis. Price 2s. An extremely simple and rather pretty little song. Key C; compass, E to F.—*Look Down from your window, Dearest.* Song. Composed by Richard Harvey. Price 2s. Described as "a song of Seville," and as an example of the serenade class, is not devoid of the elegance and graceful melody which are so essential to success in this class of composition. Keys D and F; compass, C to E.—*Her Dream.* Song. Words by Edward Oxenford. Music by Felix Argent. Price 2s. A dainty love song, with a pleasing air and neat accompaniment. Key D; compass, D to E.—*At Heaven's Gate.* Song. Written and composed by R. Randolph Arndell. Price 2s. Assuredly one of the most charming songs recently published. The narrative is daring, but exceedingly well told; and the melody and accompaniment are beautiful, especially the latter, which is very skilfully elaborated. Key D flat, changing to F; compass, D to F.—*Arise, my*

Love. Words by Sinclair Dunn. Music by Edward Jakobowski. Price 2s. An excellent song, that will be most effective when interpreted by a tenor voice of average power. Key D, changing to G; compass, D to G.—*Lullaby.* Words and music by Mabel Bourne. Price 2s. The extreme simplicity and prettiness of this lullaby, in which a "sweet babe" is prominent, will doubtless win it many friends. Keys E flat and F; compass, B flat to E flat.

RANSFORD & SON, 2 Princes Street, Oxford Circus, London, W.

Sunny Showers. Caprice Caractéristique. By Seymour Smith. Price 1s. 6d.—*Woodland Rambles.* Morceau de Salon. By Seymour Smith. Price 1s. 6d. The above will be found admirably adapted for tutorial purposes, being sufficiently strong in musical interest, and not too difficult of execution to attract young pianists.—*Twelfth Night. Olde Englyshe Danse.* By Seymour Smith. Price 1s. 6d. Our young friends will be delighted with this charmingly quaint movement, which we cordially commend to their favourable notice.—*Granada. Moorish March.* By Ed. Jakobowski. Price 2s. Since the great success achieved by the celebrated *Turkish Patrol,* few compositions in this particular class have been published possessing more genuine merit than the *Granada;* and it may safely be said, that it only requires to be known to be thoroughly appreciated by all classes of pianoforte players.—*The May Lily. Gavotte.* By Willem Vandervell. Price 1s. 6d. This is one more addition to the large number of gavottes that are by no means distinguished either by melodiousness or originality. —*Gavotte and Musette.* By Ludwig Schumann. Price 1s. 6d. A distinctly clever and musicianly piece, which should become a favourite with players of good taste.— *Old-Time Memories.* Song. Written and composed by H. Elliot Lath. Price 2s. A pleasing and easy little ballad, with a waltz chorus that is somewhat above the usual in point of musical quality. Key G; compass, D to E.

C. B. TREE, 132 Petherton Road, Highbury, New Park, London, N.

Sunbeams. Song. Words and music by G. Hubi Newcombe. Price 2s. An expressive and artistic love song that should win many admirers. Key G; compass, D to F.—*Euphorbia.* Waltz. By Ernest Spencer. Price 2s. A capital and very danceable waltz. The time is well marked, and several of the movements are more than usually attractive.—*March in F.* By Arthur Harvey. Price 2s. A showy and clever composition. Not at all difficult, and well worth playing.—*Gavotte in D.* By Ernest H. Wadmore. Price 1s. 6d. There is a freshness in this charming piece that is all the more welcome, seeing that the great majority of gavottes recently issued are sadly lacking in that desirable quality.

HENRY KLEIN, 3 Holburn Viaduct, London.

A Shilling and a Kiss. Jacobite song. Words by Frederic Wood. Composed by Henry Pontet. Price 2s. The well-known historical fact of the handsome Duchess of Gordon enticing Highlanders to join the rebels in 1745 by the irresistible inducement of a kiss, accompanied by the usual token of good faith in the more substantial form of one shilling, has been taken as the *motif* for a song that is likely to win an appreciable measure of popularity in

Scotland. The composer has made a commendable effort to grasp the true spirit of Scottish melody, and with considerable success; while the composition, as a whole, albeit simplicity personified, does not lack the genuine native ring which characterises our favourite national ballads. Keys C and A flat; compass, E to G.—*A Shilling and a Kiss. March.* By Ernest Travers. Price 1s. 6d. A transcription of the song of the same title, which makes a simple and tuneful pianoforte piece.—*Dream on.* Song. Words by Oonagh. Music by Henry Klein. Price 2s. A beautiful and refined song that should never fail to be most effective when sung with feeling and expression. Three keys—E flat, F, and A flat; compass, C to E.— *I'll send Thee, Love, an Offering.* Song. Words by Oonagh. Music by Henry Klein. Price 2s. An unpretentious and extremely sweet little love song, with pretty words, and an air and accompaniment that are at once pleasing and appropriate. Key E flat; compass, D to E flat.

"MAGAZINE OF MUSIC" OFFICE, 34 Paternoster Row, London, E.C.

The Princess of Thule. Words by L. J. Nicolson. Music by W. A. Collisson. It is by no means an uncommon complaint among vocalists of all classes that the number of really meritorious songs—or, in other words, songs with the slightest claim or pretension to intrinsic worth as musical compositions—published nowadays, are few and very far apart. A pleasing task is, therefore, assigned us in bringing to the notice of our readers the appearance of one that honestly deserves a distinguished place in the repertory of all singers of cultivated taste in song music; and by those musicians, to whom the ephemeral prettiness of the modern ballad is but scant and enervating fare, the artistic and comprehensive beauty of *The Princess of Thule* will be at once appreciated. The love of the young Princess for the land of her birth is told by Mr. Nicolson in lines whose poetic force and fire are very far removed from the insipidity of the conventional drawing-room song; and no higher praise can be given the composer than to say the music is worthy of these beautiful verses. Mr. Collisson displays much science and perception of effect in imparting to his charmingly fresh melody and accompaniment a local colour that is singularly appropriate to the weird grandeur of the "lone land of the mist." The song is a delightful one, and we cordially recommend it to all our singing friends. Two settings can be had. Keys G and E flat; compass, D to G sharp.

⁎⁎ Where there are two or more settings, the compass given is that of No. 1.

Musical Gossip.

New music, and matters of interest for notice in this column, should be addressed, EDITOR, *Musical Treasury,* 11 N. Bridge, Edinburgh.

"BRITAIN'S THOUSAND MEN" is the title of a song just published by Messrs. E. Köhler & Son, Edinburgh. It is dedicated to the heroes of Abu-Klea, and the words (by Mr. Joseph Macdonald) have a stirring patriotic ring about them. These, in conjunction with the thoroughly appropriate music of Mr. J. O. Murdoch, cannot fail to commend the song to singers who are on the outlook for a suitable addition to their *repertoire.* One of our popular local singers, Miss Effie Goodwin, has already sung

"Britain's Thousand Men" with great éclat. The title is a healthy rebound from the *England* this, that, and the other thing, which is so offensive to Scottish ears.

THE announcement that M. Gounod has been sentenced to pay Mrs. Weldon £10,000 damages has caused a great sensation in Paris. In the *Matin* appears an account of a conversation on the subject between M. Gounod and an editor of that journal. After expressing bitter regret that he had wasted so many years in England with Mrs. Weldon, M. Gounod explained that he believed he had found in her an apostle of musical art, and an enthusiastic admirer of his works. As to the judgment just pronounced, M. Gounod called it "simply monstrous." The calumnious article which was attributed to the inspiration of M. Gounod was, he affirmed, not seen by him until two months after it appeared, when it so irritated and annoyed him that he was on the point of demanding satisfaction in the usual way from its author, M. Albert Wolff. The judgment of the English tribunal could not, he affirmed, be executed in France; and if Mrs. Weldon should attempt to get it ratified by the French courts he should look forward with confidence to the issue. He had not put himself to any trouble in regard to Mrs. Weldon's suit; but the Directors of the Birmingham Musical Festival, where "Mors et Vita" is about to be produced, had simply instructed Mr. Lyttleton to appear, so that judgment might not go by default. M. Gounod declared that he should not now go to Birmingham to conduct the first performance of "Mors et Vita," and would, indeed, never again set foot in England.

MR. CARL ROSA speaks our language as perfectly as if he were born a Briton. But when under the influence of strong artistic excitement, he lapses into the most extraordinary pigeon English. So when the popular manager was called before the curtain, after the production of "Manon" on Thursday, to bow to as cordial a burst of cheering as ever rang through Drury Lane, certain wickedly disposed friends and admirers of his in the stalls yelled at him for a "speech." Mr. Carl Rosa then delivered himself somewhat as follows :—

"Ladies and Gentlemen,—I haf the honor now to inform you that M. Massenet the composer he haf not yet come for England in consequence to-night of illness as was expected. Under these circumstances I shall telegraph you that he haf received this the opera with great success if you will allow me and I think dot is right."

And then the audience went merrily into renewed cheering. Mr. Carl Rosa is the most deservedly successful of all opera managers; but he really should not prepare his speeches in advance.

THE difficulties under which Italian opera managers nowadays labour can hardly be appreciated by the outsider. Miss Nevada was, for instance, paid at the rate of £200 per night until she consented to accept half that rate for a few performances in the American provinces. Madame Patti has received from Mr. J. H. Mapleson since November last no less than £35,200. Madame Patti was to receive at the rate of £800 per night for two nights a-week, the services of Signor Nicolini being, of course, thrown into the bargain. Signor Nicolini was, however, not obliged to sing in every opera, but only in those which contained a suitable part, and he was to sing with no other prima donna save Madame Patti. Madame Patti was to have at least a week's notice of the dates selected, and her repertory was to be made out by her and determined upon by agreement. "La Traviata" was, moreover, to be exclusively kept for her in New York, and she was to have

the right of the first two performances of "Lucia." Article 10 says that for every representation Mr. Mapleson shall pay Madame Patti £800, either directly after the performance or next day at latest, and whether Signor Nicolini take part in the performance or not. Article 11 deserves to be quoted—"Mr. Mapleson shall defray all travelling expenses incurred by Madame Patti, Signor Nicolini, and their suite, supplying a first-class railway car, exclusively intended for Madame Patti's occupancy, with attendants, cook, &c." If Madame Patti were indisposed, Mr. Mapleson was to be entitled to no damages, and if Signor Nicolini were indisposed, Mr. Mapleson to deposit £4,800 before Oct. 15. Madame Patti's name was to be at the head of all bills, &c.; and, lastly, Madame Patti and Signor Nicolini were to be free from the necessity of attending rehearsals, "Madame Patti being the sole judge of the utility of taking part in a rehearsal."

THE other day Signor Arditi got into hot water from a Chicago audience, because he had forgotten to provide the band parts of "Home, sweet home," which Miss Emma Nevada interpolated after the mad music in "Lucia." Miss Nevada sang the song nevertheless, and can therefore cordially be congratulated for her artistic feeling. On the last night of the season a Chicago audience of ten thousand persons called upon Madame Patti for "Home, sweet home" in the prison scene in "Faust." Madame Patti declined, but sang the melody after the opera. To staid British audiences this sort of thing may seem funny; but to a people who applaud a vocalist who introduces "Nearer, my God, to Thee," in the church scene in "Faust," the incongruity of "Home, sweet home" in the prison scene is not particularly striking.

SOMEBODY has played off a cruel practical joke at Sir George Grove's expense. It seems that a letter, purporting to come from Sir George Grove, was sent to a certain musician at Malvern, saying that the Royal College of Music had conferred upon him the degree of Mus. Bac. A notification was also sent, to be read in the parish church, and, finally, patterns of a hood were despatched. The notice was duly read in the parish church on Easter day, when the musician appeared in church in all the glory of his new hood. The hoax was complete. Its success seems to show much misapplied inventive genius on the one hand, and hopeless credulity on the other.

SEEING what the number of military bands in this country is, and to what a pitch of excellence many of them have attained, the tax-payers may fairly congratulate themselves on the small sum they are called on to contribute towards the cost of military music. The entire sum that is to be rated for band expenses this year is £10,000, a sum which will not go far towards defraying the actual cost of the regimental music.

SIR JULIUS BENEDICT, now recovered from his dangerous illness, has resumed his professional engagements, and will give his annual concert about the middle of June.

THE programme of the Birmingham Festival, to be held during the last week of August next, runs thus :— Tuesday morning. "Elijah;" Tuesday evening, Mr. F. H. Cowen's new cantata, Mr. Prout's new symphony, Mendelssohn's violin concerto, played by Señor Sarasate, the Overture to "Tannhäuser," &c. Gounod's "Mors et Vita" will be produced on Wednesday morning; and the programme for the same evening includes Mr. Anderton's cantata and Mr. A. C. Mackenzie's violin concerto. The

"Messiah" is to be given on Thursday morning; on Thursday evening Dvorak's cantata, "The Spectre's Bride," will be produced, followed by a miscellaneous selection, including an orchestral selection from "Tristan und Isolde," Dr. Bridge's hymn, "Rock of Ages," and the third "Leonora" Overture. The programme of Friday morning will consist of Dr. Stanford's new oratorio and Beethoven's "Choral" Symphony; and the festival will be brought to a close on the same evening by a repetition of Gounod's new work.

The Tonic Sol-fa College annual meeting at Exeter Hall, on May 19, was an enthusiastic re-union. There was a proposal made to erect a scholarship in the College in memory of the esteemed and earliest Tonic Sol-fa teacher, the late Mrs. Stapleton.

MDME. CHRISTINE NILSSON.—The action brought by Mdme. Christine Nilsson against the estate of her late husband, M. Rouzaud, for the recovery of a sum of £9,960 sterling, which she had advanced to him during his life-time, came on for hearing before the First Chamber of the Civil Tribunal of the Seine. The money had been sunk in the purchase of a share in a stockbroker's business, of some landed property in France, and of Russian bonds and Panama shares. The case was adjourned for a week. M. Rouzaud was a stockbroker's clerk without fortune when he was married, in 1872, to the celebrated singer, who had saved £32,000. Mdme. Nilsson was, according to the marriage settlement, to retain complete control of her own money. M. Rouzaud died about three years ago in a lunatic asylum. We are informed that if Mdme. Nilsson gains her case she intends to make a present of the money to the married sister of her late husband, her motive in bringing the action being to prevent the large sum in dispute from falling into the hands of the other members of the family.

THE AGE OF SOME COMPOSERS AND MUSICIANS.—Pergolesi, when he died, was 26; Schubert, 31; Bellini, 33; Mozart, 35; Mendelssohn, 38; Weber, 39; Chopin, id.; Herold, 42; Schumann, 46; Donizetti, 50; Cimarosa, 51; Adolphe Adam, Sacchini, and Traetta were 52; Glinka and Benedetto Marcello, 53; Gordigiani, Lulli, Méhul, and Luigi Ricci, 54; Beethoven and Paganini, 56; Morlacchi was 57; Boieldieu, 58; Thalberg and Hummel were 59; Jommelli and Corelli, 60; Asioli, Boccherini, and Halévy, 62; Petrella was 63; J. S. Bach, 65; Félicien David and Alessandro Scarlatti were 66; Pauer and De Bériot, 68; Berlioz was 69; Pacini, Durante, and Viotti were 71; Meyerbeer, Piccinni, and Sarti were 72; Gluck was 73; Domenico Scarlatti, Orlando Lasso, Handel, F. E. Bach, and Salieri were 74; Spohr, Paisiello, Padre Stanislao Mattei, Mercadante, and Monteverde, 75; Rossini and Spontini, 76; Lesueur and Haydn, 77; Muzio Clementi was 80; Porpora, Rameau, and Cherubini were 81; Mayr was 82; Zingarelli, 85; Auber, 89; and Coccia, 91.

WHEN SOME LYRIC COMPOSERS BEGAN.—When he commenced his career as a lyric composer Lulli was 39; Handel, 20; Pergolesi, 24; Jommelli, 23; Gluck, 28; Piccinni, 26; Sacchini, 24; Paisiello, 22; Grétry, 24; Mozart, 12; Zingarelli, 16; Salieri, 20; Cimarosa, 23; Cherubini, 20; Fioravanti (Valentino), 21; Méhul, 20; Paër, 21; Lesueur, 21; Boieldieu, 18; Mayr, 31; Spontini, 22; Weber, 14; Morlacchi, 19; Rossini, 18; Auber, 30; Meyerbeer, 21; Pacini, 17; Herold, 24; Coppola, 23; Donizetti, 20; Mercadante, 24; Ricci (Luigi), 18; Bellini, 22; Halévy, 28; Petrella, 17; Ricci (Federico), 26; Wagner, 23; Glinka, 32; Verdi, 26;

Pedrotti, 22; Gounod, 33; Ponchielli, 21; Gomes, 22; Massenet, 25; and Boito, 26.

SIGNOR ARDITI, when he wants to persuade his orchestra not to attend to his hasty remarks, but when he is calm to look out for squalls, this is how he puts it: "When I tell, I means nothings; but when I nottell A-a-a-h!"

MUSICAL MANNERS.—Those now fashionable gather-ings known as "At Homes" are of frequent occurrence. At most of these, music plays an important part in the evening's entertainment. At some, indeed, it is the only means adopted for this purpose. We need not now pause to inquire whether this is a good thing for music or other-wise, but, seeing that it is the practice, it might naturally be thought that there is in music a something which so captivates all listeners—the learned and the ignorant—as to banish for the time all other ideas. But is this so? Do we not all recognise the truth of what the genial author of "John Bull and his Island" says, when he informs his fellow-countrymen that in English society the commence-ment of music is the signal for general conversation to begin? A progress in musical education is a matter of almost daily boast, but here we have a friendly critic who, with one observation, makes us begin to wonder whether we have advanced or not. It is some consolation to be able to reflect that there can be no doubt that the behaviour of our public audiences has shown palpable improvement of late years. Conversation in our concert-rooms is happily becoming a rarity, and at the opera the largest audiences sit in quietness through long acts, where less than ten years ago the interruptions would have been both frequent and noisy. In passing, it may be added, that it does not seem altogether unreasonable to look for a day arriving when the selfish practice of entering a concert-room after a performance has begun, and leaving before it has ended, to the great disturbance of the majority present, will have almost disappeared. But why is it that so many seem to leave their love of art and manners in the place of public performance? Why, in private circles, is the hour of music turned into one of inattention and a general exhibition of discourtesy?—for by what other phrase can be termed the extraordinary custom which permits of one person being selected for the ostensible purpose of amusing a roomful of people who take no pains whatever to attend to what is being played? No doubt one cause of this much-to-be-deplored state of things is the fact that, in spite of a real spread of musical education, our social gatherings still contain—and for that matter it may be supposed always will—a number of individuals whose love of music is small, and their knowledge of it less.

BALLAD POETRY.—It is recorded of Aldhelm, Bishop of Sherborne at the commencement of the eighth century, that he could find no mode of commanding the attention of his townsmen so efficacious as that of standing on the bridge and singing a ballad which he had composed. Certainly the ballads of a nation hold a distinct and important place in its literature, and can be made the vehicle for inculcating the highest morality and the loftiest sentiments. In the early ages of our own country, minstrels sat in the courts of kings; and bards, by their impassioned strains, incited the warriors to battle. The Saxons had their ballads, and the brave actions of Here-ward, who lived in the time of Edward the Confessor, were sung throughout England. A fragment still survives of a ballad composed by Canute the Great, as, sailing by the abbey in the Isle of Ely, he heard the monks chanting their psalms and anthems. The ballad or song of Roland was chanted by the minstrel Taillefer before the battle of Hastings, to excite a martial spirit in the Normans. The spirit of our ancestors still survives in the song on Athelstan's victory at Brunanburgh; while the heroic ardour and undaunted courage of Englishmen of a later age are immortalised in such ballads as "The Battle of Otterburne" and "The Hunting of the Cheviot."—*From Illustrated British Ballads,* Part I., for March.

Dramatic Gossip.

EDINBURGH.—ROYAL LYCEUM THEATRE.—During the past month the very best of theatrical fare has been provided at the Royal Lyceum, under the lesseeship of Messrs. Howard and Wyndham. In the first place, there was Sardou's "Fedora" (with Miss Clara Villiers in the title *rôle*)—a play whose strength of incident and cogency of construction suggest no question as to the reason of its popularity. Then Madame Modjeska submitted four of her best known impersonations, and was enthusiastically received during her stay. Her *Rosalind* exhibited certain short-comings, as well in conception as in expression, which were all the more readily observable, perhaps, from the frequency with which the character figures on the British stage; but, in her *Adrienne Lecouvreur,* her *Constance,* and her *Mary Stuart,* she showed the possession of such a wide range of histrionic expression as entitles her to a foremost place among living actresses. Next come Messrs. Bruce and Robertson's "Caste" Company. The interval of time which has elapsed since the comedies of the late T. W. Robertson has been performed has wrought its changes on the company, but the representations given were in most cases fully adequate. Mr. Younge's *Old Eccles* in "Caste," was probably the feature of the visit. Last week the Compton Comedy Company presented the cream of their repertory, including "Davy Garrick," "The Rivals," "Money," "Comedy of Errors," and "The Road to Ruin." The management have arranged an uncommonly attractive list of prospective engagements during the summer and autumn months. Among the more important are Mrs. Langtry, Miss Mary Anderson, Mr. J. L. Toole, and Mr. Edward Terry. A company will appear in a few weeks at this theatre in Mr. Pinero's "The Magistrate," which has proved a prodigious success in London, and is generally admitted to be one of the funniest comedies of modern times.

ROYAL PRINCESS'S THEATRE, EDINBURGH.—A capital start was made last month at the south side house with the clever comedian, Mr. Edward Righton, who appeared with his company in an exceedingly amusing comedy, entitled "Twins." The brunt of the work fell upon Mr. Righton, who, in the dual impersonation of a venerable and dignified bishop and a shrewd London writer of a highly diverting type, played with abundant comic power, his efforts being received with hearty applause and laughter. Byron's "Daisy Farm" was next on the bill, but, notwithstanding the fact that, being its first appearance in Edinburgh, considerable interest was taken in the production of the comedy by the author's numerous admirers, the general verdict was decidedly unfavourable, and its success more than dubious. Although not ab-

solutely devoid of the ingenious construction and neatly turned repartee that distinguish the works of the favourite dramatist, "Daisy Farm" has many weak points, the more conspicuous being certain incongruities of dialogue—pathos and puns coming together in the most bewildering fashion —that go a long way to deprive the play of any chance it might otherwise have of winning the sympathy and favour of the onlookers. In the following week Mrs. Deering, an American actress, made her first bow before an Edinburgh audience in a new version of "East Lynn," which, however, cannot be described as an improvement on the original play. "The Danites," a drama of considerable power, and containing several most ingenious and interesting situations, is this week attracting fairly good houses. Many of Mr. M'Neill's prospective engagements are, we believe, of more than usual importance—an announcement that will give satisfaction to his many patrons, who will doubtless look forward with interest to the good things in store for them.

THE ART OF SINGING AND ITS DIFFICULTIES.

As it is generally admitted that the path of knowledge is thorny, the student of singing cannot expect his way to be made easy, or rose leaves to be strewn under his feet; yet, the voice being a natural gift, people often do expect this, and either do not take into consideration at all the time and especial training required for its development, or they think that by some mysterious process they can attain the maximum of effect with the minimum of labour. To a superficial observer, considering the simplicity and perfect *naturalness* of really good singing, it does seem strange that, given the organ of voice, natural resonance chambers to enhance the tone, and lungs to breathe with, that the same result should not at once be arrived at. In forming this hasty judgment, he would lose sight of two simple truths: *First,* That, by the natural perversity of our human nature, the most simple things are the last that we discover, and consequently that we cannot attain to the smallest amount of good without obeying the inevitable law of work; *Secondly,* That every germ of life, though spontaneous, requires growth, and, in order to grow, must be supplied with the necessary conditions. These are the merest truisms, and should be as widely known as they are wide in their application; but there is a great tendency to shirk the truth, and to treat the question of voice training apart from the principles of law and common sense. This error is to be found not only in the superficial observer and his class, but amongst professors of singing and those who ought to know better. Earnest students have been often mystified by much unscientific talk about "voice production," "making of certain notes," &c., whereby it would appear not only that each professor has a magic method of winding up the organ, tuning it and arranging it in registers, but is infallibly certain that he, and he alone, possesses the secret. Since the voice is a ready-made musical instrument, it is undoubtedly certain that nothing can "produce" it, and all that the teacher can do is to develop to the highest extent the natural resources. For this purpose he requires the perfection of musical "ear" and critical judgment to recognise the artistic possibilities of a voice when he first hears it, to watch its growth, guard it from faults, preserve it from overstraining, and bring it to its highest possible perfection. For this he must study the individuality of the singer, and the special order of his talent, not employing a cut-and-dry method with uniformity of treatment as if he were drilling a regiment, but adapting the mechanical means to the requirements and capability of the student. Surely the difficulty and honour of such a task are great enough without pretending to do what is not possible!

To return to the difficulties of singing from the standpoint of the pupil, I will suppose him or her to have commenced regular study, having escaped the danger of an incapable teacher on the one hand, and a narrow and bigoted one on the other. He now finds the real difficulty of what before seemed so simple; he learns how to breathe, to attack, to sustain, to diminish; how to place each note that it may be pure in tone and quality— all the things which require the minutest care and attention. It is peculiar to singing that the ear needs cultivation in order to detect faults, the throat and ear being so intimately connected that even a very musical student may not hear defects of intonation and quality in his own voice which he would discover at once if played on an instrument or sung by another person. In addition to this it often happens that there is some trick or peculiarity to be got rid of which occasions great trouble to the teacher, and is a provoking obstacle to the pupil. Arrived at a stage when the study of songs is advisable, there is a host of difficulties to be encountered, especially if the language chosen be English. The impure vowels, with awkward combinations of consonants, calculated rather to hinder than help the emission of the voice, require the most skilful management. Well sung, they delight the ear, but it too often happens that even cultured persons who speak English perfectly, yet sing it with an indistinctness and vulgarity of accent that is quite distressing. Beside the mere mechanical means, and technical exercise of the voice, with its necessary auxiliaries, the organs of speech, the musical feeling and knowledge of the student must develop in order to attain the perfection of phrasing required of a great artist, and admirable in any singer. A professor who is æsthetic (I mean in its original sense, *i.e.*, perceptive), will always divine what is beautiful and poetic in music, and foster it in his pupil. Since to be a great singer, or a great teacher, means so much, and to be excellent even to the extent of mediocre powers implies such work, one wonders at the hardihood of people attempting to take up music as a profession, without possessing the special qualifications, or being prepared to submit to the necessary discipline. There are no short cuts to knowledge. Formerly our great singers were "to the manner born," sons and daughters of actors and singers, reared amid the traditions of their art, familiar with its technicalities, and under no illusion as to its difficulties. Singers in these days, who enjoy greater facilities, are apt to attempt in a few months what can only be attained by years of patient study. Growth in nature is gradual, and forcing, far from adding to its strength and durability, will infallibly injure it. It is possible, by a special effort of memory, and a judicious selection of facts, to condense a large amount of mere information, as by the process known as "cramming" for an examination ; but these facts, hastily learnt, are all too easily forgotten, and, where retained, require to be sorted and arranged before they can be of practical use. If this mode of study is of doubtful benefit in those departments of learning where the mind is only required to be receptive, a mere mechanical instrument for taking in facts, is it likely to succeed in developing the perceptive faculty, or in

training such a delicate organ as the human voice? Since this gift of song is a beautiful living germ which only requires the right conditions to make it grow, it is the skilled teacher who supplies the greater part of these conditions, and, properly nourished, the germ will expand into the fulness of strength and beauty, and will be, to all around, a source of pleasure and delight.—G., *Musical Standard.*

MUSICAL MEMORIES.

HENRY STEEDMAN.

It occurs to me that some of your readers may possibly feel interested in some old musical memories of one who can no longer call himself young, save in spirit. About 1840 I first made acquaintance with Henry Steedman, a name entirely unknown to most of your readers, I doubt not, but which *deserves* at least to be better known, as I trust to show ere quitting the subject. He was in the bookbinding establishment of a respectable bookseller in Edinburgh, under whom I served my apprenticeship to that profession. Both he and I were naturally fond of music, and about 1845-6 he attended a class of Dr. Joseph Mainzer's. He very soon, however, perceived the fallacy of the *"fixed do"* theory, and applied his mind to trying to master the *"movable do"* system. At this time Mr. Curwen's system, now so popular, was scarcely known in Scotland, and Mr. Steedman worked mostly on the plan of the *old* "sol fa," as taught by Mr. B. Gleadhill and others, although without being a pupil of Gleadhill's. In 1848 he had become a good reader of music, and also had a fair knowledge of theory, while I also had progressed pretty well upon the *staff* notation—knowing almost nothing then of sol-fa—and we frequently interchanged views. Many young men came about Steedman, asking him questions about theory, to which he replied intelligently ; and, as he had a happy knack of explaining himself in a clear, homely, and graphic style, he was often requested to form a class for tuition in music. This he declined, but at last was so importuned that he consented upon condition that William Hardie, a pupil of Gleadhill's and a good tenor singer, who died some fifteen or twenty years ago, and myself would lend him an occasional help, which we willingly agreed to do. Preliminaries thus agreed upon, we (or, rather, the committee, for we were but *honorary* members) hired a small room, rejoicing in the pretentious appellation of "East Thistle Street Hall ;" and on the first night I think about twenty male members were enrolled, some of whom brought their sisters and sweethearts. Steedman's *modus operandi* was to devote about an hour to practising scales and theoretical instruction upon the "black-board," after which the class sang over a few simple choruses, chiefly in three- and four-part harmony. In singing Steedman himself led the bass, Hardie the tenor, myself the alto, and one of the best voiced tenors or sopranos the melody. Homely as this method was, it was wonderfully successful, and not the less so that he encouraged any who chose to go forward and sing duets, trios, &c., before the class, thus encouraging many young singers of both sexes to go forward and gradually raise themselves into prominence. That much of the seed thus sown was good is certain. One of the best local teachers in Edinburgh was a pupil of Steedman; so was George Hastie, now Curator of the Royal Institution, Edinburgh, and celebrated as an intelligent and enthusiastic antiquary, and many others, some of whom became choirmasters and choristers in various places. The society (known as "The Thistle Solfeggio Club") at one time was nearly 200 strong, and for several years met in the large room under the Edinburgh Music Hall. From 1848 till about 1853, Steedman continued to act as conductor. He then retired in favour of Messrs. W. Howard and F. W. Bridgman, as conductor and accompanist respectively. Alas for the mutations of time! My dear old friend, Henry Steedman, died in March, 1884! May he rest in peace. — D. BAPTIE, *Musical World.*

THE INVENTIONS EXHIBITION.

THE Second Division deals exclusively with music, and is divided into three sections, relating to musical instruments and appliances constructed since 1800, to music engraving and printing, and to old instruments, pictures, scores, besides a cornet room designed exclusively for practical trials. In reference to this most interesting division (designated Group XXXII.), it may be well to quote *in extenso* the indications given in the Official Guide of the kind and nature of the exhibits under this special head. For the moment it is sufficient to say that the great Central Gallery is now one vast bazaar of musical instruments, contributed by nearly every maker of native or foreign reputation :—

"Since the year 1800 the improvements imported into instruments have been innumerable. The full orchestra, such as we know it, is practically the same as it was at the end of the last century, but of the instruments composing it the string group alone remains unchanged. The flute was perhaps the first to undergo reformation, and in the hands of Boehm became what we now know it. He altered the bore, the position and shape of the holes, the venting of the holes, the action of the keys, and the fingering. Other inventors have endeavoured to apply the inventions of Boehm with partial success to the double and single reed instruments—viz., oboe and bassoon, the clarionet, basset-horn, and bass clarionet. In brass instruments the principal changes have been the introduction of keyed instruments, such as the Kent bugle and ophecleide as substitutes for the older type of sliding brass instruments, represented by the trumpet and trombone. Keys have, however, been superseded by the invention of piston valves, which are now applied to cornets, horns, euphoniums, and bombardons. The greatest musical invention of the present century is the pianoforte, which has been developed by a series of improvements out of the old harpsichord. By the introduction of tension bars, metal frames, and other improvements, it was found possible to endow this instrument with a power which was formerly thought unattainable. Some idea of the strains put upon the frames of modern grand pianofortes may be gained from the fact that the total tension in the strings of some of these instruments attains the figure of about twenty-five tons. The Exhibition is very rich in its collection of pianofortes, which illustrate all the recent improvements in frames, soundboards, and actions. The organ, also, has undergone many mechanical improvements in the present century, the principal of which are the pneumatic and electric methods of lightening touch, the methods of regulating the pressure of wind, the application of mechanical instead of hand power for actuating the blowing apparatus, and the introduction of the pneumatic tubular transmission which enables the player to be seated at a considerable distance from his instrument. The harmonium and the American organ are instruments of comparatively recent introduction."

It may be mentioned that the Loan Collection of old instruments, &c., the third section of the division, which is now being placed in the upper gallery of the Albert Hall, is not yet ready for inspection, and will not be open to the public for a few days to come.

Honourable Mention Certificate.

Corresponding Class.

For conditions, see "Star" for October, 1884.

FIRST COURSE—HARMONY.

Text-book—Novello's Music Primer, "Harmony," by Dr. Stainer.

LESSON IX.

Chap. VII., page 56.—Study paragraphs 95 and 96.

Note.—The information contained in par. 95 may appear to be of little importance, but it is, nevertheless, valuable, and if borne in mind by the student, it will assist him considerably to write smoothly. The changing of all the notes of a chord, when a change of figure occurs, such as 5 to 6, frequently produces jerky and abrupt progression. Neither must par. 96 be passed over without any consideration, or the pupil may find himself at fault in some of the figured basses that follow.

Study paragraphs 97, 98, 99, with examples.

Note.—This is a point deserving of some attention. The explanations and examples given by Stainer will doubtless be perfectly clear to the student; and "False Relation" is often so offensive to the ear that he will do well to keep those rules in mind. If the student will remember, in using a chromatic semitone, to give both of its notes to the one part, and, at the same time, let neither of its notes (nor their octaves) be heard in any of the other parts, he will escape *entirely* the bad effect of "False Relation." There are, of course, occasions when this rule may be broken through; but, until the pupil has had more experience of the subject, it will be better to be as rigid in his treatment of chromatic notes as possible.

Exercise.—No. IV., page 64—harmonise, tell the modulations, and name the chords. Also 48 and 49, Appendix—harmonise.

Exercise.—Write a single chant in the key F sharp minor, containing the dominant seventh chord in all its inversions.

J. C. G.